The Backpack is a simple, engaging story on the power of personal choice to improve your life. Tim shares his wisdom and practical steps on what it takes to fully succeed in life.

—Jon Gordon, best-selling author of *The Carpenter*

Tim Gardner tells this memorable and clever story with humor, genuineness, and plenty of well-earned wisdom. Rare is the author who can challenge the best of leaders to be better and Tim cuts to the core of what leaders need to hear. Read it. And in the process, you'll learn more about *The Backpack* you carry. You will be better for it.

—Flip Flippen, founder and chairman of the Flippen Group, best-selling author of *The Flip Side: Break Free of the Behaviors that Hold You Back.*

As the founder of a company whose only legacy is to develop leaders, I've learned that self-awareness is one of the … if not the … most important leadership skills. *The Backpack* tells a powerful and practical story on how you can grow in this critical yet often missing trait; one that is required to be a successful leader.

—David P. Lindsey, founder and chairman of DEFENDERS, Inc., founder of the Super Service Challenge and trueU.

The *Backpack* is an inspiring book that comes out of the mind and heart of a remarkable individual as well as a great storyteller. It is an engaging, challenging book that addresses the need for us to understand, own, and tweak our behaviors to be better, to love better, and to positively impact others. It is a call to "conversion!" As you read the stories you will say, "That's me." You will become more self-aware and challenged to be your best you … guaranteed!

—LTG (Ret) R.L. VanAntwerp, 39 Year Army Veteran and Leadership Coach, former Commanding General of the US Army Corp of Engineers

The Backpack is one of those precious literary gems that all of us can relate to. It represents a loving and gentle reminder to slow down, pay attention, and take responsibility. Since reading it, I find myself sharing the engaging messages and metaphors with others in general conversation and each time we laugh and reflect on all of the people we've whacked with our backpacks. I finished the book with tears in my eyes, a full heart, and empowered to pay greater attention to how well I am loving others.

—Andrea Butcher, president of HRD Advisory Group

Dr. Tim Gardner remarkably frames personal improvement through self-awareness in *The Backpack*. Simple, high-impact, and timeless tools to help people grow personally and professionally are explained in actionable nuggets through his storytelling. I've had the privilege to personally be coached by Tim as well watch him head leadership development in multiple organizations with thousands of team members. I've consistently seen relationships healed, talent unleashed, and confidence grown.

—Marcia Barnes, founder and CEO of Valve and Meter

the backpack

how to
understand and manage yourself
while loving others along the way

tim a. gardner

WILEY

Published by John Wiley & Sons, Inc., Hoboken, New Jersey.
Published simultaneously in Canada.

For general information on our other products and services or for technical support, please contact our Customer Care Department within the United States at (800) 762–2974, outside the United States at (317) 572–3993 or fax (317) 572–4002.

Wiley publishes in a variety of print and electronic formats and by print-on-demand. Some material included with standard print versions of this book may not be included in e-books or in print-on-demand. If this book refers to media such as a CD or DVD that is not included in the version you purchased, you may download this material at http://booksupport.wiley.com. For more information about Wiley products, visit www.wiley.com.

Library of Congress Cataloging-in-Publication Data:

Names: Gardner, Tim A., 1959- author.
Title: The backpack : how to understand and manage yourself while loving others along the way / Tim A. Gardner.
Description: Hoboken, New Jersey : John Wiley & Sons, Inc., [2019] | Identifiers: LCCN 2019003714 (print) | LCCN 2019006155 (ebook) | ISBN 9781119576419 (Adobe PDF) | ISBN 9781119576396 (ePub) | ISBN 9781119576372 (hardcover)
Subjects: LCSH: Conduct of life. | Self-consciousness (Awareness)
Classification: LCC BJ1589 (ebook) | LCC BJ1589 .G37 2019 (print) | DDC 170/.44—dc23
LC record available at https://lccn.loc.gov/2019003714

Cover Design: Wiley
Cover Image: © Paolo_Toffanin/iStock.com
Border: Wiley

Printed in the United States of America

10008998_032519

To my parents:
Mom, who inspired my love of books and education.
Dad, who imparted a strong work ethic and
a commitment to do what's right.
Thank you for everything!

Chapter 1

Jon was late.

Again.

And he was ticked off at everything and everyone.

Again.

He had already decided that this was *not* going to be a good day.

His flight was scheduled to leave at 8:05 a.m., which meant he wanted to be completely ready, backpack in hand, and walking out the door at 6:05. This was the plan he had laid out in his head the previous night. It would give him plenty of time to get to the airport, check in at valet parking, breeze through the TSA Precheck lane, grab a second cup of coffee from his favorite airport hotspot, and be at the gate in time for another look at his newly finished presentation and early boarding with his Frequent Flyer status.

As Jon had slipped into bed the night before, he had smiled. It was good to have a plan.

It was better to have status.

It was now 5:41. He was sitting on a stool in his closet, not smiling, and rubbing his aching foot. He was thinking about how he had not yet accomplished anything. This was not the plan at all. "How did this day get so screwed up already?"

As is often the case, it began with the alarm.

Jon's perfect plans had included a 5:15 wake-up, a quick change into his workout clothes for 25 minutes on the elliptical, and 15 minutes to shower, shave, and dress. This should have left him a short buffer to pour a cup of coffee to go; snatch a banana from the basket that his wife, Grace, always kept stocked with fresh fruit; and grab his carry-on and backpack as he headed out the door. He had even laid out his clothes, packed his bag and hauled it downstairs the night before so he wouldn't wake up Grace digging through the dresser early in the morning—as had happened many times before. He was proud of himself for being so thoughtful. All was set in order to get to the airport right on time.

The perfect plan.

He had heard his smartphone alarm at 5:39. That wasn't a phone glitch; his last thought before trying to close his eyes was, "Hey! I've packed my bags ahead of time. That gives me an extra 15 minutes to sleep!" Impulsively, Jon had changed the wake-up time. He had justified that this extra sleep would make up for the time he had spent returning emails in bed—a task he had not accounted for in his planning. Now, even in his slow retreat from slumber as his feet hit the floor, he wondered where the other nine minutes went.

What didn't come slowly was his irritation over the fact that his plans were quickly going south.

"Okay, 10 minutes of a workout is still better than none. And I can shorten my shower," he reasoned, as he unplugged his phone from the charger and headed for the bathroom.

"Ouch!" He tried to muffle his shriek as his bare foot stepped directly on top of the hard rubber bone that Dumbledore, their dog, had dropped by the bed immediately before joining Grace and Jon, panting and wagging his entire body as he nestled in for the night. (Where the 65-pound fuzz-ball slept when their 10-year-old daughter, Annalise, was gone to a sleepover was still a bone of contention.)

This bone happened to be the one of those dental toys with spikes! Jon glanced quickly at Grace's side of the bed, still not wanting to wake her, though that was becoming less of a concern as he thought, "Why does she have to let that idiot dog sleep with us, anyway? She knows I need to get in six hours of sleep and Dumbledore could make that difficult if not impossible!"

"From now on that dog is going in the crate whenever Annalise is gone," he half-mumbled. "And what the heck were they thinking when they bought that assault-weapon dog toy? Obviously not about me!"

Jon limped into the bathroom and not-so-quietly closed the door.

As usual, his morning had started in a state of hurry. "Do it now" and "do it next" lists dominated his thoughts. Tension and stress already filled his body. The list of people and things he blamed for his quickly deteriorating morning was growing rapidly. The emotions he was carrying both in his brain and in his body were so fired up that he was rushing through his morning, completely unaware of anything around him.

So now Jon sat in his closet—with his aching foot and angry face—tense, frustrated, and more than 20 minutes behind what had been the perfect schedule.

No sense of wonder.

No sense of joy.

No sense of peace.

Not a grateful thought in his head.

His only sense was of pain. And his only thought was, "Why do all of these things always happen to me?"

As Jon rubbed his foot, he stared in confusion at the second thing he had stumbled over that young morning. In the middle of his limping-hurry to the bathroom, he had tripped over anther object that, for some reason, was sitting in the middle of the closet doorway.

"How in the world did I get taken out by my own backpack?"

Chapter 2

Sofia had been "short called" two hours ago. She didn't mind. It was a clear expectation of the job—one that she planned for. In her job as a flight attendant, so many unplanned things occurred on a daily basis that she was used to being prepared for the unexpected. Some of her fellow flight crew members viewed their reserve-line schedule as days off with a possibility of being interrupted by work; Sofia viewed them as work days with a possibility of being interrupted by a day off.

Over the years she had learned that realistic expectations were the key to avoiding disappointment, be it at work or home. She knew that if she packed a reserve day with activities that she or her family were looking forward to, only to have it all blown up because she was called to work, then they would all be let down at best. However, if she expected to work on a reserve day and chose to spend her pre-work time getting a few things done or taking one of her grown children to lunch, then didn't get called in? Well, that was a bonus!

Sofia even had to admit that sometimes *not* getting called into work could be a disappointment. Her two kids were grown and out of the house and her husband, Scott, worked a normal schedule. This made her job all the more appealing. She was sure to meet interesting people, serve them, and keep them safe. It was a joy to her. She even viewed the occasional upset passenger or the people who treated her like a glorified waitress as welcome challenges.

"There's always a reason why people act like they do," she knew. "Even when they themselves don't know the reason."

On some short calls, Sofia had to pop out of bed and be at the airport on an hour's notice. On this fine morning, she had two hours' notice. "Another bonus," Sofia thought gratefully. This allowed her to not have to short-circuit her morning routine. She never skipped it; she simply had a modified version when the predictably unpredictable occurred. On occasion, Sofia entertained the thought of getting up at 3:00 a.m. on days she was on the early reserve line. That would mean she had time to get in her full "day prep," as she called it, just in case the call came.

It didn't take much effort for Scott to persuade her to change her mind, especially since a 3:00 a.m. wake-up time meant going to bed at 8:00 p.m. the night before. They both knew their unhurried morning routines were important because that time set the tone for the entire day. However, when discussing radical changes like this, Scott would say something like, "Let's not go all climb-Kilimanjaro crazy," or make some other goofy retort.

Scott was a dyed-in-the-wool believer in discipline and commitment, but "lighten up, have fun, and don't take yourself too seriously" were among his core values. Scott and Sofia both knew that a clear awareness of your personal core values was critical for a purposeful, meaningful life. They helped you govern your thoughts and choices throughout any given day.

Why would they be important for companies and organizations and not individuals and families?

Sofia smiled as she thought of Scott. He was another thing to be grateful for. Daily.

She was also grateful for all she had learned over the years and, more importantly, applied to her life. For example, Sofia knew that it didn't matter if the short call came with one or two hours notice, waking her from a dead sleep or interrupting lunch with a friend, her expectations were always aligned with reality, so her reality would not become disappointment. She had learned a formula in a relationship book and it had always stuck with her: If $E > R$, then $R = D$.[1]

If your expectations (E) are greater than your reality (R), then your reality (R) will equal disappointment (D).

Now, with her Rollaboard and backpack in tow, Sofia made her way toward the security line, knowing she had plenty of time to stop at the crew lounge before she needed to be at her gate. She enjoyed not rushing. Even more, she enjoyed the freedom of not worrying whether or not she packed everything she needed. Maybe one day she would get to thank the passenger[2] who shared his packing method with her on a leg from NYC to Indianapolis. She had adopted it as her packing SOP, standard operating procedure. In this case, it was simply a checklist of what she needed to pack. She had an SOP for a one-day trip, two-day trip, three-day trip—whatever size trip. She always used it and therefore rarely forgot to pack anything.

Sofia smiled as she looked around at all of the faces loading luggage onto the X-ray belt. She could tell that some were worried, some relaxed, some stressed, some joyful, some impatient, some moving slowly, and some moving fast. She noticed all of the different backpacks in various states of wear and tear, all carrying many different things.

With over 20 years in the travel industry, Sofia knew that there would be some folks who thought they had things in their backpack that were not there, and there would be other people who had items in their backpacks of which they were completely unaware. She remembered one passenger who had pulled a self-help book out of his backpack. He had never seen the book before and, boy, was he ticked off! Someone had apparently snuck the book into his backpack, insinuating it was something he needed to read. The irony, which helped Sofia remember the event, was the title of the book: *Self-Awareness: The Key to Anger Management.*

As she moved through the security line, Sofia watched the passengers. What adventures where they headed for? Had they packed everything they needed? Would what they were carrying in their backpacks create joy—or cause problems?

She smiled again. There was a quiet confidence that came from being aware of your baggage. That thought made her smile even more. Everybody had baggage; life had taught her that some people were aware of it and others were not.

Sofia enjoyed the personal peace that was rooted in the conscious awareness of exactly where every item in her backpack was located. This is also why she preferred a backpack over the tote used by most of her colleagues; all of the extra compartments helped her stay aware of where everything she needed was located—for the most part, anyway. There was always room for growth.

On every trip, Sofia consciously worked to improve her overall awareness of her backpack.

Chapter 3

R oyce Jefferson Smith sat a small corner table, enjoying his third cup of coffee and half-reading *The Wall Street Journal*. His waitress was a kindhearted, single mother of two who called everybody, *Hon*. She filled his coffee cup while simultaneously asking, "Would you like a refill?" and she continuously offered a smile in spite of the fact that it was before 7:00 a.m. The name on her ID badge was Hope.

Royce knew these things about her because over the last 45 minutes he had simply asked. He thought, "It's easy to go through life so wrapped up in our own worlds that we forget to be friendly."

That was not something he ever wanted to forget.

Royce smiled at being called, "Hon." It reminded him of nicknames used by the waitresses for customers at his granddaddy's cafe when he was a kid: Hon, Sugar, Junior, and Lucky. They had given him all sorts of nicknames, too. Now, deep into adulthood, there were still not too many people who called him Royce.

For as long as he could remember, which, frankly, was a very long time, the majority of folks called him Buddy.

Like most kids from the south with that name, it stemmed from a slightly older sibling who couldn't quite say the word *brother*. Buddy didn't mind. He liked it better than his given name, which he liked to say had been passed down for "longer than an elephant could remember." It went back generations ago, to a time when his family fled Germany under royal oppression. Their family's trouble had started when his grandfather with a whole lot of "greats" in front of it fell in love and wanted to marry a young woman in the monarch's family. A commoner wanting to marry a royal. With the marriage forbidden, they fled to Texas and, like many immigrants, changed their name in an attempt to better fit in. Schultz became Smith, and Royce, which in English origins meant *royalty*, was the name they gave to their firstborn son.

Buddy knew that names mattered. He knew the family he came from mattered. He also knew that in his day-to-day life, he was much more of a buddy than a royal.

By every airline standard, Buddy was a frequent flyer; but he preferred to think of himself as a frequent friend. People flew for a multitude of reasons to reach a greater multitude of places. The one thing they all had in common was that they needed a friend to give them encouragement and help them grow on this journey of life—even if that potential new friend was unaware of that need.

"Fact of life," Buddy thought. "People need friends like a rooster needs the dawn."

Buddy knew that every single encounter with every single person on every single day presented a single opportunity. He could make their day better, worse, or have no impact at all. Buddy preferred making things better.

Whenever possible, Buddy frequented the airport restaurants that were hometown originals, like his grandpa's place. While there, he enjoyed sitting just inside the fence that the restaurants used to cordon off their claim of terminal property; it gave him a great view of all of the travelers lugging all of their baggage. People-watching was the reason for his partial attention to the financial news.

Buddy smiled as a young couple who had just rushed past his table simultaneously stopped and turned backwards with a panicked look, their eyes quickly scanning the crowd. Buddy smiled because he knew what they were looking for—he was hiding behind a potted tree just five feet from his table. Apparently a couple rushing to catch a plane expected their young son to keep up with them. And, apparently, the little boy got tired of trying to keep up. The boy's red and blue Spider-Man backpack stuck out like a neon bar sign in a desert, which made hiding difficult.

Buddy thought "apparently" because he had learned over the years not to think that something was obvious, especially when it came to other people. One of the things Buddy knew to be true was that no matter how good you are at reading faces, you can never read someone's mind. Many relationships have been destroyed on the hill of the mind-reading stance of, "I know exactly why you did that!" Though Buddy's interpretations were right more often than not, Buddy still thought the wiser mindset was to avoid concrete conclusions before you had all of the facts.

The little boy looked straight at Buddy with a look on his face that said, "I'm being sneaky. Please don't tell. This is fun." Buddy gave him a big grin, a nod, and a wink. He turned toward the little boy's parents and with the boy now peeking at them around the tree and the parents catching the kind eyes of the gray-haired man at the corner table, Buddy shared the location of their worry with a slight nod of his head. Buddy was pleased to see that, instead of getting upset with the boy, the parents realized that it was their own hurriedness that had caused him to fall behind.

Too many people, Buddy knew, were so focused on rushing to where they were going that they missed the important parts of where they were, or worse, the things they value that they were leaving behind.

It was that hurriedness that caused so many folks to forget to be friendly.

Many people love to people-watch. Some to judge, some to laugh, some to learn. To Buddy, people-watching was not entertainment; it was an education. And to him, it was more science than art. It was a conscious decision to study people and all of the baggage they dragged with them.

"Okay . . . it was a little entertaining," he admitted to himself. "People are all different . . . and people are all the same," Buddy thought. Everybody has a unique experience of life simply because we walk different paths, grow up in different situations, and see life through a personal perspective. Yet we all have so much in common. People have similar needs, like a purpose to live for and a desire to love and be loved. We have similar responsibilities, like stewarding our lives and caring for our neighbors.

And we all have struggles.

As has been said by many, life can be hard.

That is why we all need friends.

All different and all the same. It was like the announcement at the airport baggage carousel: "Many bags look alike. Please check your bag to make sure you are picking up the right one."

"Fact of life," Buddy thought. "All of us have baggage that we carry with us like a backpack. And every one of us needs a friend to help us with that backpack."

Chapter 4

Jon sat on the stool in the closet, still rubbing his spiked foot and his throbbing toe. "How in the heck did my backpack end up in the doorway of my closet?" In the planning last night, he was reasonably sure he had not put it there; though if he had, it would not be the first time he had forgotten he had done something in the midst of rushing around.

But that thought didn't last; his dominant brain pattern was how all of this was making him angry.

As Jon let his foot recover, he unlocked his phone to glance at his email; it was out of habit more than anything else. He was not surprised to see that a dozen new emails had shown up in his box overnight. However, he was surprised to see that one of them was from his boss.

"Finally," Jon said in another muffled yell! His boss had sent the updated budget numbers to their entire team. More accurately, they were the updated reductions. Each department was being given a percentage they needed to cut from their budget because the company had failed to meet revenue forecasts for two quarters in a row. "He sure was working late last night," Jon thought. He read through the numbers and then started banging out a quick response.

He wanted to make sure that his boss, along with the rest of the team, knew that he was working early.

Jon hit reply-all and started to type. But as his mingled emotions rolled on, he decided to send a quick email to his buddy, Alec, who had been on the distribution. "Wow! I didn't think PHB would ever get us these numbers. Either his golf game was rained out or happy hour was canceled!" PHB was Jon's private nickname for his boss, referencing the Pointy-Haired Boss from the comic strip *Dilbert*. It made Jon smile every time he used it. He thought his boss was identical to PHB, oblivious to most of what was going on in the company and never taking responsibility for anything that went wrong. In Jon's mind, nearly every problem and limitation he had at work was PHB's fault.

Jon hit send.

He went back to finish the email to PHB and the team. "Where did it go?" he wondered, his frustration still on high. Jon hit reply-all to restart the email, assured his boss and everyone else on the chain that he would, in fact, have his revised numbers in by the time his plane landed. "First to reply," he half-smiled.

He knew his aggressiveness was resented by some of his colleagues. That made him smile even more. "Too bad if they get run over and left in my dust. That's their fault."

He hit send again.

Jon knew that all of the numbers he would need for his work on the reductions were already on his new laptop in his backpack. "At least I know for sure where my backpack is now," he thought.

Jon glanced back at his phone. Five more minutes gone. "Crap!" The positive thoughts toward his boss for sending him those numbers were quickly turning into being ticked off at him for sending them now. "Why can't he email me when I actually have time to respond?"

"Where did my time go?" Jon wondered, again forgetting the sequence of events that led up to now. As he was formulating new plans and making up excuses for what had happened so far, he thought of skipping the workout. Then he remembered that he had committed to himself and Grace that he would work out four days a week and he already missed the last two days due to similarly chaotic mornings. "I can still get in a few minutes and tell her I worked out and make it out the door in time to make my flight," he thought. "My Precheck and frequent flyer status will help me make up lost minutes."

Jon tossed his phone on the hamper and went to find his workout clothes. "At least one thing is where it is supposed to be." A quick change and Jon grabbed his backpack to take it downstairs and put it by his suitcase. He retraced his steps out of the closet, back through the bathroom, and into the bedroom. He knew he should be quiet, but his thoughts were more focused on getting to the basement for his pretend workout.

That focus on what he needed to do in the next few minutes now led him, again, to miss what was right in front of him. Objects unwittingly present in hand, thoughts somewhere in the future, feet in a hurry, Jon quickly stepped through his bedroom door—and knocked his daughter Lilly over with his swinging backpack.

"Lilly?!" Jon said, half-concerned and half-frustrated due to yet another setback in his schedule. "Are you okay?"

"I heard loud noises," his four-year-old sniffled, rubbing her sleepy eyes and clinging to her blanket. Jon was trying to reflect back through the morning, thinking, "I was very aware of how much noise I was making! She must have heard something else. It couldn't have been me!"

"It's okay, Lilly. Go on back to bed. Daddy is getting ready to head to the airport." He thought, "I simply do not have the time to take her back to bed myself. I do not have time for her at all right now."

"Lilly, honey, come up here." Jon was surprised to hear Grace's voice. "You can sleep on Daddy's side of the bed." Lilly rushed in and jumped into bed, quickly snuggling in next to her mom. Sleeping with Mom and Dad was a special treat and the invitation, as Grace knew it would, took her mind off of what had just happened.

"Not only did he trip himself up," Grace thought, reflecting on every muffled comment that she heard carelessly fall from Jon's lips, "but he just took out his own daughter with his backpack."

Chapter 5

The commotion at one of the screening lines caught Sofia's attention as soon as she passed through the crew-only security gate. This was beyond the normal physical bag search. This scene involved airport police and a not-so-happy, not-so-quiet traveler.

If experience was an accurate teacher (which, with a willing student, it nearly always is), Sofia figured that a passenger had forgotten they had a handgun in their backpack when they ran it through the X-ray machine. In this day and age, it was amazing to Sofia how frequently that occurred. Knowing her stats, Sophia knew it happened over 2500 times in U.S. airports in the previous year. When she was younger, Sofia and her father frequently went to the gun range, and she had grown up with a strong sense of the responsibility of gun ownership. What concerned her was how people seemed so unaware of how dangerous such weapons can be. Her father drilled into her that you must know where your gun is at all times, and it must be locked up, secured, or holstered. He used to say, "Thousands of lives are destroyed every year by the excuses of, 'I forgot my gun was there,' or 'I didn't think it was loaded.'"

In the travel industry, stories of items found in the backpacks of unaware passengers were legend. For some travelers, ignorance was the issue. They actually thought that the items confiscated from their backpacks were okay to bring on a plane: souvenirs like a machete or WWII hand grenade, a bottle of lighter fluid for a traveling camper, and all variety of martial arts weapons. They simply did not stop and think about what might be in their backpack that could be considered harmful to other people.

Other travelers suffered from what Sofia called "the problem of familiarity."

When someone carries a backpack every day to work, on trips, and even on vacations, it becomes a very comfortable part of who they are, and they come to believe that they always know what is and is not in their backpack. More to the fact, they usually don't even think about the contents at all until they go looking for something they need. Most of the time, people are not conscious of what they keep in their backpacks all of the time.

Frequently, someone else discovers the contents, either accidentally or intentionally. Sometimes that's okay, but usually it is not. Finding an unexpected travel pack of tissues or a bottle of ibuprofen can be a nice surprise. In these cases, you can help someone by digging deep in your backpack. By contrast, discovering a potential weapon that you are not in control of could be deadly. What if a kid went through the backpack and found a forgotten gun or a tactical knife?

"Focused reflection is key," Sofia thought. It was part of her morning prep. Taking the time to sit quietly and become aware of what is going on both inside and outside of you. And when it comes to packing, it is taking the time to ask and reflect on the answers to two important questions. The first is: "Do I have everything I need packed away in my backpack?" And, just as important is: "Do I have anything I don't need that I need to take out of my backpack?" Sofia was convinced that slowing down and reflectively answering that second question could eliminate the vast majority of those 2500 incidents.

Sofia was also well aware of the fact that the manner in which a passenger responded to an unexpected discovery in their backpack was critical to what happened next. The screening agents were given a great deal of latitude and, for the most part, they wanted to treat travelers with kindness.

People who were truly repentant and took ownership of what was in their backpacks without being defensive or upset were generally allowed to continue on with their travel plans—without the banned object, of course.

But those who were visibly upset, unapologetic, arrogant, blaming, or even abusive? Those who tried to justify or explain away their own anger that was triggered when someone found something buried deep in their backpack? They got to walk away with the police in some nice silver bracelets, often paying huge fines for what was found in their backpacks.

Sofia thought, "Thousands of lives are also destroyed by attitudes that center on phrases like 'It's not my fault' or 'How dare you blame me!'"

You must reflect and know what's in your backpack at all times.

And humbly take responsibility, at all times, for what's in your own backpack.

Chapter 6

B uddy observed a young man walking slowly down the middle of the corridor with a backpack looped over both shoulders and his eyes gazing intently at his phone. He was most likely a college student—and definitely someone who is going to unknowingly inconvenience a lot of people as he meanders through the airport. And he is probably someone who will be labeled by others as a person who doesn't seem to care too much about his impact on his fellow travelers.

That wasn't a judgment; it was merely a fact.

Three different people had already been forced to adjust their course to avoid a collision with the young man because he was completely unaware of most things going on in his surrounding environment.

Buddy was reasonably certain that if you asked the young man where his backpack was, he would have to pause and think and then proceed to feel for one of the shoulder straps to assure himself that it was actually on his back.

Partial attention deficit disorder, continuous partial attention, or chronic attention deficit were what his friend Truman, a psychologist, may call it. They pretty much all meant the same thing to Buddy: people not consciously and fully aware of what and, even more, who, is around them.

In the military, they call it *situational awareness*, which is being fully aware of one's surroundings.

Similarly, self-help gurus talk about the importance of *being fully engaged*.

People who practice meditation call it *mindfulness*.

Christian disciplines describe it as *thoughtfulness*.

Not being an idiot was how Buddy's dad described it.

Buddy called it being human—at least being a human who is fully embracing and fulfilling their humanity.

Buddy didn't blame people. At least not people who had never been challenged to become more aware of their surroundings. Those challenges of awareness normally begin in childhood when parents encourage their children to move out of the pathway of other people, be it at the store, on a sidewalk, or in their own home. For example, awareness is knowing that if you carelessly leave your backpack in the middle of a walkway it is going to unnecessarily inconvenience, if not hurt, others. Developing other-consciousness or other-awareness is a critical part of growing into a healthy adult.

And, as Buddy was observing right now, many adults still had a lot of growing to do.

What Buddy had less patience with was people who simply did not care how they were negatively impacting others—and were self-justified in their not caring.

Buddy had recently read in a science journal that the average level of empathy in humans today was lower than it was 30 years ago. In the leadership-development genre, Buddy knew that much had been written in the past decade on the vital importance of empathy, that powerful ability to understand the feelings of others, and the positive impact it can have on those you lead. "Heck," Buddy thought, "it has a powerful impact on everyone in your life's path."

But in Buddy's mind, there was something more important than empathy: compassion. Empathy is critical to caring for others, but the simple reality is that a person cannot fully empathize with everybody they meet.

Buddy had grown up poor. He didn't know he was poor. His family lived in an old farmhouse, complete with fans for the summer and a fireplace for the winter. He had three meals a day (even if it was things they grew or hunted) and clothes on his back ordered straight from the Sears, Roebuck catalog. As a child, they didn't seem poor to him; they always had everything they needed.

As an adult, Buddy had traveled to multiple sites in Mexico—Tijuana, Ensenada, Mazatlán and others—where families lived in tiny shacks, often smaller than the size of Buddy's bedroom. The homes had dirt floors with walls made from scrap wood and roofs covered by worn plastic tarps. There was no plumbing, no electricity, no doors or windows.

Buddy may have been poor—but he couldn't empathize with being that poor.

But Buddy could care; he could demonstrate compassion and do something about it. That was why he had partnered with Homes of Hope, an organization that built homes for poor families in Mexico. He had worked on teams to build 10 homes. His compassion for others had moved him to do that. His psychologist buddy, Truman, called compassion a "higher-order emotion." People can choose to care even when they can't say, "I know how you feel." They can still choose to demonstrate nurturing behaviors.

People with compassion choose to care if their backpack is getting in anyone's way. And people with compassion choose to do something about it. Yes, Buddy could agree that human empathy had decreased over the years. He also believed that people's general level of compassion had decreased. People were more concerned about defending and protecting themselves than caring for others.

Buddy looked back at the young man whose backpack continued to get in others' way. Some of those who passed him were visibly angry. Others were simply annoyed. Buddy saw lots of rolling eyes and disgusted head shakes. Some seemed to accept it as part of traveling and just buzzed around him. Buddy saw one apparently angry woman make a comment to him, which of course he didn't hear through his headphones.

"Looks like we still need people to learn to love their neighbor just a little bit better," Buddy thought and smiled. "You simply have to get out of yourself and be aware of your neighbors and their needs."

Buddy knew that from his own personal experience. His second nickname as a child could have been "Selfish," "Self-centered," or simply, "Self," since that was who he was focused on more than anything else. Oh, he could be nice, kind, and respectful. Saying "Yes, sir," "No, ma'am," and the like were always required. But when it came to relationships, he was definitely more of a taker than a giver.

Boy, had he come a long way. And he thought, "I've still got a long ways to go."

Buddy saw his waitress, Hope, still smiling, slowly making her way back toward his table. She was moving slowly only because she stopped to make sure that everyone she passed was taken care of.

Buddy believed that people who focus on taking care of others would be taken care of themselves.

He got up, grabbed his old backpack, and nonchalantly stuck six $50 bills under the edge of his plate.

As he passed Hope, Buddy smiled, nodded his head, and said, "Thank you, hon." She smiled back with a "You are more than welcome, dear." He headed for the gate with a to-go cup of coffee Hope had handed him on his way out.

He heard a shriek of surprise as he disappeared into the chaotic lanes of people. Buddy smiled. He had learned that the more you stepped out and practiced caring for people the more you actually cared for people. It was how you could increase compassion and empathy. Hope's certain happiness made him happy. He continued to grin as he hooked his thumb under the strap of his old, tattered, and very comfortable leather backpack.

Chapter 7

"**I** woke up when your alarm went off . . . the first time," Grace said as she stood in the kitchen adding creamer to her coffee. Jon had headed out the door 10 minutes earlier with barely a goodbye and even less of a kiss. The conversation now continued on their phones. "What?" Jon said, half-defensive, have inquisitive. "What do you mean the 'first time?'"

Then it hit him. The lost nine minutes. He had hit snooze without realizing it. "Well," he stuttered, "if that stupid dog hadn't slept with us, I would be rested enough to get up on the first alarm!" Grace was wise enough to let that comment go—for now.

Jon had made it to the highway and was now battling traffic he had not expected this time of the morning. But, he realized again, his later departure was part of the issue; it had added morning traffic to his route. All of this caused him to mentally relive his morning in his head. And it was not a fun experience. After he had leveled Lilly with his backpack, Grace had given him some very unsolicited and undesired counsel.

"Honey, I think you should skip your workout and get in the shower. You're already scrambling around like a Labrador on linoleum. Slow down, take a shower, double-check your backpack, grab a banana, and hit the road." "But . . ." Jon started to say, but Grace continued. "And oh, before you get mad at me for there not being bananas on the island, they are in the bag on the kitchen table. I realized as I was lying awake that I had not finished unpacking the last grocery bag after I got off the phone last night because I got wrapped up getting Lilly to bed." Grace's sister Theresa had called just as Grace was unloading the car.

In that moment, Jon recalled, all he could think to do was drop his backpack and head back to the bathroom for a shower. Now, after 15 minutes in the car, he had time to reflect on Grace's comments. She had told Jon on multiple occasions that he needed to pay better attention to the people around him, especially their emotions and their moods. She pointed out that he often confused that with simply paying attention to their words.

"But when people attack with their words, I aggressively push back," Jon had said more than once.

"Childish," he had heard back. More than once.

Multiple thoughts were bouncing through Jon's head at the same time, all critical of Grace, and all justifying himself. First, he was bothered by the fact that Grace frequently let herself get interrupted by phone calls and visits from friends and family members. "Why can't she stay focused and get things done instead of being interrupted by a useless phone call from Theresa? How hard can it be to put the bananas in the basket?" Second, he wondered, "What was with that phrase, 'Before you get mad at me?'" It wasn't like he randomly got mad at her without any reason. And what really bothered him was the fact that she had been awake during his whole disaster of a morning. "How long had she been lying awake, anyway? And why didn't she get up and help if she was so concerned about his schedule?"

Confused about what he wanted to say, all he managed to come up with was, "Why didn't you get up if you were awake?" He thought that was the nice way to say what he was thinking, even though his tone came out accusatory.

"Jon, when you're bouncing around like a one-eyed dog in a smokehouse, I have learned to stay out of your way. You can be the sweetest thing, babe, but when you are stressed about being late, finishing some project, our finances—heck, stressed about anything, you can be a pain where-I-don't-need-pain. Your agenda changes by the nanosecond, you speak impulsively and without thought, you're critical of everything around you, and there is not a kind word or gesture anywhere to be found. You've danced on me with all four feet when you are not mindful of your own frustration level, so I've become mindful to stay off the dance floor."

Grace's quick wit, down-home Southern humor (inherited from her dad), and her not-so-subtle truth-points were one of the things he loved about her—some of the time. This was not one of those times. Anger rising yet again, he started to say, "Grace, I do not have time for this," but then realized that in the slowing traffic, all he had was time. Her slightly humorous truth-telling had pulled him out of his "it's all about me" mindset more than once.

This time, he simply stayed quiet while the morning continued to replay in his head.

After his shower, things did not improve. He couldn't find his phone, so Grace had to call it before he could find it where it had fallen behind the hamper; he hadn't remembered even setting it there. He banged around the bathroom trying to find personal items that he had sworn were already in his shaving kit. And to top it all off, he had once again forgotten where his backpack was after he had dropped it in frustration by the bedroom door.

Grace had also told him the reason his backpack was in the middle of the closet doorway. Jon was right that he hadn't left it there. Grace had gotten up in the middle of the night to check on Lilly and their eight-year-old son, Jaxx. On her way back to bed, she noticed his backpack sitting on top of Dumbledore's crate. Knowing he would never find it there, she had set it where he couldn't miss it.

Jon's brain battled between being thankful and simultaneously annoyed at her thoughtfulness.

"Honey, today is going to be a great day for you. I know you have to work on those job cuts, but I know you'll do the right thing. And you will be awesome in your presentation!"

"The presentation!" Jon thought. With all of the hubbub of the morning, he had forgotten all about the primary reason for the trip. He had spent the last hour before bed tweaking what he had already spent hours on and getting used to his brand-new laptop. His wife's encouragement made him feel a little better. He was sure he would wow the new client with energy and enthusiasm—and his slide deck.

"I will be thinking about you today, babe. And remember, with Annalise at the sleepover, I'm dropping Jaxx and Lilly at Theresa's. That's what she was calling about last night. After that, I'm driving down to Waco to meet with my new client, so I will be out of pocket most of the day. I look forward to hearing how everything went later tonight."

Grace's concern and care for him, regardless of his mood, brought some sense of comfort to him. He took a deep breath and tried to assure himself he would still make his plane. And he felt bad about judging her for being on the phone with Theresa. He tried to cover it up by saying, "Thanks, sweetie. I will call you when I get settled into the hotel after dinner."

"Sounds great. Love you!"

"Love you, too," Jon replied.

He was still stinging a little from Grace's words about his being impulsive, critical, and less than nurturing. Was that really how he came across?

He glanced at his backpack sitting on the passenger seat.

"At least I know what's in my backpack!"

Chapter 8

S ofia sat in the crew lounge enjoying a cup of hot tea, having already read over her trip sheet and tucked it into her backpack. She still had 30 minutes before she needed to meet the rest of her crew for the preflight briefing. Flight crews used the lounge for everything from napping to changing clothes to grabbing a snack. Sofia used it for a final mental and physical recharge: reading, journaling, or doing the latest *New York Times* crossword puzzle.

Sofia was an introvert, at least as much as one could be. She knew that even psychologist Carl Jung, who coined the terms "introverted" and "extroverted," didn't believe that people were purely one over the other. Throughout the course of her life, Sofia had come to learn, understand, accept, and embrace exactly what that personality trait meant. To her, at least.

She had come to understand the behaviors that she needed to choose to act upon and develop in order to maximize her impact, both at work and at home.

When the topic came up—which seemed to be frequently—people were surprised that an introvert had chosen to be a flight attendant. It was a common misperception that all introverts were shy, reclusive, and reserved, and therefore did not function as well in people-oriented professions.

Especially one like Sofia's where you were constantly meeting new people.

Stereotypes, she knew, were unfair and dangerous. She had read that more than half of the people in the public-speaking profession were actually introverts as described in the classic definition. Sofia didn't know if that was completely true or not, but it made sense to her. She enjoyed being on the microphone, not only explaining the critical safety rules to passengers, but also making them laugh.

One of her favorite lines was: "We'll be dimming the lights in the cabin. Pushing the light-bulb button above your seat will turn on your reading light. However, pushing the flight attendant button will not turn on your flight attendant."

That one always cracked her up. Almost as much as, "If you don't know how to use a seatbelt, you probably should not be out in public unsupervised."

Sofia knew that being an introvert or extrovert wasn't as much about the job that you did as it was about how you psychologically prepared and recharged. Thus, the quiet time before the proverbial storm of people. She drew energy from "me time," which included personal reflection, processing ideas in her head, and even mentally rehearsing her shtick for the airplane microphone.

Introverts and extroverts were individually responsible for knowing themselves and taking care of themselves. She also knew the importance of personally owning that truth. It's like the airport P.A. announcement to always be responsible for your own bags.

Sofia enjoyed the new flow of people into her life; however, she enjoyed her job even more when she was on longer flights, which presented opportunities to have more in-depth conversations with both passengers and fellow crew members. She loved finding out more about people's families, their passions, and their travels. She rarely had to ask stale questions like: "So, what kind of work do you do?" That was too easy and often mundane. And she knew that too much casual chitchat could sap her strength. Asking more personal details kept her engaged and energized.

And it was also a behavior that demonstrated care for others.

Sofia had also learned that after a long day, instead of heading out to a noisy bar or busy restaurant, she needed to be alone or at a quiet dinner with only her husband, children, or a close friend or two. The more extroverted recharge in crowds; the more introverted in solitude. And to be your best in any job, self-maintenance is the key.

And, as people liked to talk about people, Sofia would work to dispel another common misconception: People skills were not a natural ability bestowed upon the extroverted. Great people skills were something to be learned. There were introverts with phenomenal people skills and extroverts who were downright jerks—and vice-versa.

These were part of Sofia's Lessons for Life:

- ◆ As we grow, it becomes necessary to understand our behaviors and how they are helping or hurting ourselves . . . or others.
- ◆ Behavior is the only thing we can change.
- ◆ Listening is a skill, a behavior, and a choice.
- ◆ Demonstrating respect for others is always a choice.
- ◆ Challenging, stretching, and encouraging others in their behaviors is a choice.
- ◆ Being kind is a behavior; it is a choice.
- ◆ Even being or not being a jerk . . . is a choice.

To Sofia, it wasn't about being an introvert or an extrovert. It was about knowing yourself, being responsible for yourself, and taking care of yourself so you can be your best with family, friends, and at work.

It was about living out her core value of being kind.

Sofia's watch buzzed. Her alarm had gone off.

It was time to head to the briefing and meet the rest of her crew. Sofia closed her book and made the conscious choice to put it where it belonged in her backpack.

Chapter 9

Everybody has scars.

Life had proven that to be true.

Buddy had spent most of his twenties wandering, most of his thirties rushing, most of his forties wondering, and now, late in his fifties, he was finally enjoying. He used to wish he had gotten to that point sooner. What if, at an earlier point in his life, he had worked harder to understand himself more and love people better? What if, as a younger man, he had thought about others more . . . and himself less?

He didn't think about that often. As he learned from his psychologist friend, Truman, there are only a few things that are absolutely true all of the time. One of them is that you cannot change one iota something that happened one hour, one day, or one year ago . . . but you can make small changes each day to have a better tomorrow.

You can learn from your scars.

Truman, who Buddy called Dr. T, had taught Buddy about the power and importance of reflecting on the past without dwelling on it. Dr. T had attributed it to something Socrates had said about an "unexamined life." But the purpose of reflection was the key. Everybody thought about events from their past, both near and far. The more important question was *why* you reflected on something.

Dr. T had shared:

"Remembering happy times is a life-giver.

Repenting and amending for mistakes is a life requirement.

Regretting and learning from stupid choices is—or can be—a good life coach.

But allowing the mental onslaught of the *oughttas, shouldas* and *if onlys* is a life-stealer."

Buddy adjusted his backpack and headed on toward his gate, conscious of the fact that he needed to be aware of his surroundings and not get lost in thoughts that took him away from where he was. There was a time and a place for reflection, but that was not when you needed to be aware of something or, most importantly, someone else in your presence.

As he meandered along, smiling and nodding at those who glanced at him (knowing that the effort would cause many to unconsciously smile back), Buddy decided to stop and take a seat in a rocking chair located in the intersection at the entrance to his terminal. You could nearly always find a seat here, unlike in the area surrounding the charging stations. He still had ample time to get to his gate and he was suddenly struck by a thought that he did want to ponder for a few minutes.

Buddy had learned the hard way that a hurried life was not the sign of a disorganized schedule; rather, a hurried life was the sign of a disorganized heart. He was in no hurry to get to his gate and he did not want to hurry this thoughts.

Buddy had also learned the importance of capturing ideas while they were fresh in his mind. He didn't know why it was true but he had also learned the hard way that having an *aha* moment and not taking the time to let that epiphany sink in usually resulted in the potential learning being lost.

To benefit from an important idea, he needed to let it solidify through focused thought and then write it down. He thought about something Dr. T had told him: "The shortest pencil is longer than the longest memory."

Buddy reflected on his backpack.

His old leather backpack had been a gift from his kids. They thought it was a much better fit for his personality than the nylon-polyester pack that he had carried for years. Similar to his old saddle, his backpack was broken in, and it fit him well.

He pondered the breaking-in process.

Many folks don't realize that a horse saddle is not a one-size-fits-all piece of riding equipment. Intended use, horse fit, and rider fit are critical when choosing the right saddle. After that, there's the break-in period. On a new saddle, the leather is tight and smooth, with little contour to the body of the rider. It takes some work to comfortably fit the saddle to the rider. Buddy knew some old cowboys who took a brand-new saddle and threw it in a water trough, then strapped it on their horse and rode it till it was dry. The moistened leather molded more quickly to their body. After that, they would clean and condition it and the leather saddle would be ready to roll.

A backpack can't be broken in like that. It takes the same intentionality and care as a saddle, but it also takes more time. And the time factor was dependent upon just how intentional the user was. Daily use of every compartment and strap made those compartments and straps easier to use. Regular care of the outside, which included conditioning the leather, moved the break-in period along nicely. But most of all, you had to consciously carry it around. You had to use it.

The goal of caring for the backpack wasn't to try and keep it looking brand new. That's a reason folks constantly took their cars through carwashes or painted their homes. Working to keep something looking "like new" was an attempt to hide all of the blemishes and pretend that the very real wear-and-tear of life never happened.

It was different with a backpack.

Buddy's old backpack was the quintessential picture of distressed leather that had been well cared for, and had also been well worn. Life's miles were reflected in his old backpack.

Life, indeed, had happened.

Both backpacks and people have scars.

And just then the thought of what Buddy really wanted to capture became crystal clear. It was all about people and their backpacks. Everybody on the planet had a backpack—metaphorically, at least.

Some folks were intensely aware of almost everything in their backpacks while others didn't have a clue. Most were somewhere in between. Some folks were honest and open about their backpacks while others worked hard to hide the scars and the damage. Some folks were very careful to not carry things that simply weighed them down. Other folks carried unnecessary junk that added burdens that they were not even aware of. Some folks made sure their backpacks were not causing problems for other people while the back-packs of others were out of control, knocking things—and people—over wherever they went.

And there were still others who thought the answer was to get something completely different from what they had. These people either envied others' backpacks or kept buying new ones.

Everybody has a backpack that they are responsible for, scars and all.

Buddy smiled at his analogy.

Dr. T would be proud.

Buddy got up and continued toward his gate, looking more intently than ever before at all of his fellow travelers' backpacks.

Chapter 10

"Come on!!"

Jon was yelling at the car in front of him. Airport Drive. 7:25. Jon was confident that there would be spots at valet parking. The high cost ensured that.

The jerk in front of him going barely five miles per hour above the speed limit was the latest commuter frustration. Ten minutes earlier, Jon had been screaming at a police officer who appeared to have a couple of cars pulled over during rush hour. "Don't you understand the traffic jam you're causing?"

Of course, he yelled with his windows up.

Jon hit the gas and sped around the car, quickly pulling back in the same lane in order to catch the entrance to the parking garage.

Somehow that made him think he had gained some time.

Grace had pointed out on more than one occasion that he needed to give up trying to control other drivers.

He knew she would be disappointed in his behind-the-wheel behavior this morning. She had given him that feedback before, too.

With myriad exchanges with Grace running through his head, he suddenly remembered a conversation the two of them had a few weeks prior, after she had picked him up from the airport. Airport drop-offs and pick-ups were something Grace insisted on when their schedule had been void of one-on-one time.

"Do you know why people get angry so quickly while driving?" she had asked him after she had been honked at and flipped off by a driver she had inadvertently cut off while they were changing lanes at the same time.

"I'm sure you're going to tell me," Jon had replied with a not-so-hidden sarcastic tone. Grace consulted in corporate philanthropy, helping companies invest their capital, both financial and human, back in their communities; but she had majored in social psychology.

That fact was a love-hate relationship for Jon.

Grace hadn't missed a beat.

"It can be a variety of reasons, actually. One, whether we realize it or not, we immediately get in fight-or-flight mode when we get behind the wheel because driving is inherently dangerous. Our brain goes into a high-alert, defensive state when we pull out of the garage. Two, we all have our own set of rules for how to drive, and we get ticked-off if someone breaks one of our rules." She glanced over at him and said, "Like if someone is driving slower than we think they should."

Jon remembered the guy who was now behind him. His reflections of Grace's explanation continued.

"Another reason is what we call the anonymity factor. When we think no one knows who we are, our moral compass can blow up. It's why people love to rant and rave and review online—anonymously. Imagine if that guy who just flipped me off had pulled up and realized I was his boss. Uh-oh for him.

"And finally," Grace had said, glancing in Jon's direction, "we are notorious judgers. And we judge in a completely biased fashion. We call it attribution bias. And a type of attribution bias is the fundamental attribution error."

"Now you're just making stuff up," Jon had interjected.

"You wish," Grace had smiled. "Seriously, this one is huge. There are debates and complexities, of course."

"Of course," Jon had chimed in.

"But the foundation of the fundamental attribution error is this: We attribute other people's behaviors to internal or character-related factors while attributing our own behavior to situational or external factors."

"Now you really lost me." Jon had murmured.

"Think of the last time someone cut you off in traffic, Jon. What did you think of that person?"

"Oh, I don't know," Jon had poorly faked forgetfulness. "Maybe that they were a stupid, reckless, got-their-license-at-Wally-World-bucket-head. Or something like that." He had grinned at Grace.

"Uh-huh. Or something worse," Grace had grimaced back.

"And now," she continued, "think of the last time you cut someone off. What did you think of you?"

Jon started to say something but then stopped.

"Exactly," Grace had continued in a slightly softer tone. "The majority of folks won't blame their own behavior on their character, like you just did with the other driver. They are more likely to blame the circumstances and say something like, 'I didn't see you,' or 'I really needed to get in that lane.'"

"Sounds like you've been preparing that speech for a while," Jon had mused at her.

Grace had glanced kindly at Jon. "Babe, I want the best for you. I want the best for us. Sometimes you let your emotions get the better of you because you are unaware of them. And when you are unaware of them, it can have a huge negative impact on your behaviors. You are too quick to speak without thinking, and too aggressive when challenged; you escalate, raise your tone and volume, and get into a 'I have to win the argument' mindset. It hurts relationships with your friends, with our kids."

Grace paused.

"And with us."

Jon didn't say anything.

He was not a big fan of being coached by his wife.

He wasn't a big fan of being coached by anybody.

As he pulled into the valet lane, Jon snapped back to the present when he saw that there were two cars in line ahead of him. "At these prices, why can't they put more staff at this place?" he grumbled aloud.

His turn came.

Claim ticket and key exchange.

Going back for the again-almost-forgotten backpack, carry-on now in hand.

A minimum of words; at least from Jon. The attendant had been apologetic for his brief wait, attempting to explain that his coworker had been hit by another driver on the way into work so they were shorthanded.

Jon thought of the police officer on the side of the road. "Was that the wreck?" he wondered.

Grace again came to mind. She would definitely have shown more compassion than he did. Heck, any compassion at all would have been more than he gave. "She's just wired differently," Jon justified . . . again.

Jon was headed toward the moving walkway when he spotted a young mom with two kids—one in a stroller and one walking beside her—getting on the walkway and stopping.

This day just keeps going downhill.

"Why do people get on these walkways and not walk? And worse, why do they block others from passing?" His mind didn't stop. And the flood of all of the external circumstances, people, and pets that he had considered culpable for the blown-up morning rushed back to his head. He realized it would be faster for him to walk beside the moving walkway than stand behind the clueless mom.

As he fast-walked past them, he glanced and saw the mom had stopped because she was digging through the diaper bag for a brush and then straightening the kid's hair and clothes. "What a waste of time! Just get out of the friggin' way," Jon thought. It was more of a glare than a glance.

As Jon made it to Precheck, he saw it was a relatively short line. "Finally!" Jon thought. "Something going right." His thankfulness wasn't really about gratitude; it was more like what a victim feels when he's caught a deserved break.

Jon grabbed his luggage as it exited the X-ray, pulled up the handle of his carry-on, and slung his backpack carelessly over his shoulder. As he turned to finish the sprint to his gate, he heard the shriek of a child from behind him, so he instinctively glanced back to the main terminal.

It was the children and the mom from the moving walkway. They were in the full embrace of a man in military fatigues. Almost unconsciously, Jon paused to watch the reunion.

He felt an emotional gut-punch, like when he received feedback from Grace that deep down he knew was true. This time there was no one to push back on.

He reached up to adjust the shoulder strap of his suddenly very uncomfortable backpack.

Chapter 11

Sofia was the senior cabin crew member on today's flight and as such was responsible for running the preflight briefing and assigning responsibilities to the rest of the crew. Flight schedules, passenger details, company news, and, of course, safety updates were important parts of the briefing. But Sofia knew that taking time for the crew to get to know each other was critical as well. If the team connected well with each other, it would be a better experience for them and the passengers. Camaraderie builds synergy, and synergy builds powerful, purposeful, team-focused individuals.

Sofia could already tell that one member of the team was focused only on herself.

As they all moved from the official briefing to the preflight preparations, Sofia began to ask relationship-building questions, which, for her, was as simple as asking about someone's personal story.

"This is only my third trip since receiving my FAA certification," Collin beamed. "I have always loved to travel, and I enjoy meeting new people, so I feel this job is perfect for me. And I gotta say that I am excited about this opportunity to learn from the two of you."

Looking past Collin, Sofia could see the eye-roll from Cecelia, the third member of the crew. From the preflight paperwork, Sofia knew that Cecelia had been with the airline for seven years; from their brief conversation, Sofia also knew that Cecelia wanted to be anywhere but here. She had let it be known more than once that being short-called for this flight was a huge irritation to her.

"Heck," Sofia thought, "it is fairly evident that people in general are a huge irritation to her."

Sofia believed that Collin was sincere in his desire to learn from senior crew members and she was determined to not let Cecelia taint this opportunity. It wasn't that Sofia wanted to shield Collin from the frustrations of the job or the challenge of dealing with an irritating co-worker; every job has them and everybody needs to learn to navigate them. It was simply that she was not going to let Cecelia poison this opportunity to coach a willing learner. Sofia had learned that coachability was far more important than any behavioral constraint one may possess. She also knew that all successful leadership coaching ultimately focused on improving emotional intelligence.

Mastering the people side of every job is critical to success.

It was no surprise to Sofia that the opportunity to delve into the people side came quickly.

After a round of "things that I want you to know about me," during which Cecelia had shared nothing more than her name, tenure, and continued irritation, Collin looked at them both and said, "Can I ask the two of you a question? It's a question I've been asking everyone I've had the chance to work with."

"Of course," Sofia offered.

Cecelia responded with another eye-roll.

"What's the best piece of advice you can give me for achieving long-term success in this job?"

Surprisingly, Cecelia jumped in first.

"It's pretty simple. In this job people treat us like glorified waitresses and bellhops and believe they can poke and pull on us when they think they need something. So, you've got to learn to paste on a smile while at the same time not taking any crap. And," she looked up from where she had been inspecting the first aid and medical kits, "remember that a drink at the bar when we're done will always make it better," she ended, with a forced smile. "And that's not how you do that, Caleb!"

She had been watching Collin check and store the equipment that would be used in the safety demonstration and not-so-subtly pushed past him to take over.

"Look, it's not that hard," she told him. "Oxygen mask goes here, seatbelt goes here, and safety card goes here. For the life of me, I don't know what they teach in training anymore."

As Cecelia moved back toward the galley, oblivious to the expressions of her crew mates, she simply heard, "Collin."

"What's that?" she asked looking at the half-embarrassed, half-surprised face of Collin. "My name is Collin. You called me Caleb."

"Well, *Collin*," Cecilia snapped, drawing out his name, "I know you're new, but if you cared as much about doing your job right as you seem to care about me getting your name right, we'd all be better off, wouldn't we?"

Collin was stunned.

Sofia was not.

Even the quick change from smiling to a critical spirit didn't throw her off. She had seen it all before. Hypercritical. Over-controlling. No empathy.

All equaled low self-awareness.

Cecelia was behaving as though her way of storing the demonstration equipment was the only correct way, but the task didn't have to be done exactly one way. Unlike the one right method for inspecting the oxygen bottles and ensuring they are bracketed, full, and attached properly, there was flexibility when it came to how flight attendants stored the safety equipment that they were going to use in the demonstration.

Cecelia was simply over-controlling.

Sofia could tell that Cecelia was completely unaware of Collin's emotional state and, even worse, didn't care about it. She could have chosen to speak to Cecelia about the whole scene when Collin was out of earshot, but instead Sophia decided to use this as an opportunity to answer Collin's question while at the same time confronting behavior that was out of line.

"Cecelia, I know you are most likely pretty ticked-off that you are even here today."

"You think?!?," Cecelia retorted.

"And I do know that it can be frustrating to have to change plans at the last minute." Sofia wasn't going to explain how she prevented frustration when it came to short-calls. That kind of preaching would be like poking a sleeping bear. And this bear was already awake. To Cecelia, it would probably sound a whole lot like Sophia saying, "I'm a lot better than you."

"But," Sophia continued, "Taking it out on Collin is completely unacceptable. Taking it out on anybody is completely unacceptable."

"Look," Cecelia interrupted, "I don't see what the big deal is. He asked for advice and I gave it to him."

"'I don't see what the big deal is' usually means 'I don't care how you feel about it,' don't you think?" Sofia calmly replied.

Cecelia escalated even more, "I'm not here to be liked; I'm here to get a job done and get it done the right way. I'm tired of being the only one on these crews that cares about doing things the way they are supposed to be done."

Sofia restrained herself. She wanted to say, "Well, you're doing a pretty good job of not being liked." Instead she said, "Cecelia, I understand what you said about being a glorified waitress and passengers thinking it's our job to store their luggage. I get it; I do. Candidly, I've been in this job a lot longer than you. As all three of us know that our primary job is the safety of every soul that will be on this plane. All of the other responsibilities we have are secondary."

Cecelia continued to bang things around in the galley.

Collin continued to stare.

"And with that," Sofia continued, "can I share something that science has demonstrated will help us fulfill all of those functions better, especially the safety part?" She didn't wait for an answer. "It's possessing a strong self-awareness."

Collin was suddenly reengaged. "You mean like knowing your strengths and weaknesses?"

"That's a part of self-awareness, but I'm talking more about emotional self-awareness. It's understanding what you are feeling and why. People who are aware of their emotional state and take responsibility for managing it have better safety records; they make fewer mistakes. They understand how their feelings impact their behavior and performance, and they don't let their emotions control them. They're better with customers. They're better team members."

And then, looking directly at Cecelia, Sofia stated clearly and calmly, "And they don't stay in jobs that they don't like."

Sofia continued. "Collin, the best piece of advice I can give you for long-term success in this or any job is to develop self-awareness. Full, complete, self-awareness."

"So, let's all," Sofia emphasized, "take a deep breath and get in the emotional mindset we need to make this an excellent flight for everyone."

With that, the first passengers arrived at the cabin door, all of them anxious to find a place to put their backpacks.

Chapter 12

Boarding gates were fascinating places, at least to Buddy. He had been sitting at his gate for about 20 minutes, continuing to learn about those around him. It wasn't that he thought learning about others was more important than learning about himself. Even at the ripe young age of 59, there was, Buddy regularly reminded himself, "Much to learn in the classroom of me." But self-growth comes from self-reflection and the candid feedback of others. Public places were the laboratory for learning about life's fellow-travelers.

More than that, they were the places for developing and offering empathy to others.

Sitting around him there were all types of others.

There were people who felt that if you were not 30 minutes early, you were late. Then there were those who were happy to simply arrive before the cabin door closed. Some of those types preferred shopping or standing in the gourmet coffee line to being on time while others simply left home with the narrowest of margins. Then there was everybody in between, including those who were wired one way but, due to the nature of air travel, were pushed to navigate unwanted circumstances, for example, the people who wanted to be 30 minutes early for a connection but found themselves struggling to catch their breath as they recovered from running between gates due to a late arrival. Or the person with a longer layover who feels compelled to use every minute of their wait doing something they feel is productive. You can see that person talking on the phone, while returning email, while snarfing a deli sandwich, while charging their devices. Others were happy to nap. Or talk. Or do nothing.

Buddy found it fascinating.

Airport gates are also a place where people's anger is often on full display, fully fueled by this greatly misunderstood thing we call stress. To Buddy, this had become more worrisome than fascinating. People had forgotten the miracle, and the nature, of air travel.

Buddy recalled a fable about a rattlesnake who had been caught up high on a mountain when a cold, blue norther hit. Knowing he would soon die if he stayed where he was, the snake pleaded with a passing hiker to wrap him inside his coat and take him to safety in the warmer, lower elevations.

The hiker responded, "You're a rattlesnake! You'll bite me if I pick you up."

"Oh, no," the snake humbly replied. "If you save me, I will be forever grateful," the snake promised. "I would never bite you." So, the hiker picked him up, wrapped him in his coat, and took him to a warmer environment at the bottom of the mountain. As the hiker took the snake out of his coat and set him on the ground, the rattlesnake did, in fact, bite the very surprised hiker.

"You bit me!" the startled hiker shrieked. "You promised!"

As the rattlesnake slithered away, he turned back and wryly stated, "Why are you surprised, my friend? You knew what I was when you picked me up."

Like the hiker, airline passengers often learn the hard way. Air travel, by its very nature, always faces problems that will result in delays. Machines, computers, and people all contribute to the uncertainty. And the weather has the final say in everything. Buddy had learned to expect problems, and when there were not any, it was something to add to his gratitude list. Also on the list: the fact that a 180,000-pound hunk of metal can actually take off, travel 2000 miles in the air, and land safely. That made him doubly grateful.

Why are people surprised? Why do they let themselves get so angry? They should know what air travel is before they sign up.

Buddy's thoughts continued to roll.

The same thing could be said for driving during the rush-hour commute in every major city in the country. Or when you are going to a popular local restaurant on a Friday night. If you want the road to yourself, go to work at 4:00 a.m. If you don't want to wait at the restaurant, go at 3:30 p.m., although you have to fight the retirement crowd at that time, Buddy thought with a smile.

Many passengers, however, didn't share Buddy's flying philosophy.

A seemingly growing number of travelers reacted in surprise when things didn't go perfectly. And then they allowed themselves to get angry. And then they chose to let the gate agents take the brunt of it.

Anger had a place, but that place was not at the gate agent who had done nothing to create the circumstances.

Fact of life: You cannot always choose what happens to you, but you can choose how you respond to what happens to you. It's what the great neurologist, psychiatrist, and Holocaust survivor, Viktor Frankl, called "the last of the human freedoms." Frankl wrote, "Everything can be taken from a man but one thing: the last of the human freedoms— to choose one's attitude in any given set of circumstances, to choose one's own way."

Frankl penned those words soon after being released from the Nazi death camps, where he had lost his mother, his brother, and his wife.

"And we have trouble controlling our anger over not getting upgraded to first class or having to gate check our bag," Buddy thought. "Or merely having to wait to get on the plane." Air travel: You knew what I was before you picked me up.

He reflected on his backpack idea.

When people get angry, they almost always blame a person, or even an object, for making them angry. If a person misses their flight, it's the airline's fault. The gate agent represents the airline, so venting their anger at the gate agent is justified in their minds. If a computer doesn't do what people need it to do—and can't get it done in the five minutes the flight attendant gives passengers to power down their electronics—they get angry at the computer and the flight attendant for hurrying them. And they feel their anger is justified. No matter how ugly the reaction may look or how intensely it may be felt by others, people blame their anger and their responses on the situation and on other people.

Just last week, Buddy recalled, he chose to step in and help diffuse a situation where passengers had been asked to deplane. They had spent two hours waiting for a maintenance issue to be fixed but the repair couldn't be made. Buddy was on the plane as well. One passenger started laying into the gate agent for the whole situation. Buddy stepped in to make sure that the guy, who had already crossed the lines of decency, didn't cross the lines of stupidity.

With Buddy there, he didn't.

Buddy now reflected on one of the biggest lies that people tell themselves: My anger is not my fault or responsibility.

He thought further.

Fact of life: No matter the circumstances, everybody is responsible for his or her reactions.

Everybody is responsible for his or her anger.

Because anger comes from inside our backpacks.

And right then Buddy looked up and saw a man on the moving walkway coming towards his gate—a man who appeared to be very angry indeed, with a very heavy backpack.

Chapter 13

"I cannot believe this. I just cannot BELIEVE this is happening to me!" Jon was agitated to the point where he was, again, making these statements half aloud.

On top of everything else that had happened in this young day, Jon was now reeling from the emails and texts that were pouring into his phone. In the hurry of the morning, Jon had uncharacteristically forgotten to take his phone off of do-not-disturb mode, a bedtime condition that Grace was adamant about when he was home.

Even more uncharacteristically, Jon had not even checked his phone for messages since his call with Grace. He had been too wrapped up in himself and his frustrations to notice much of anything or anyone else. He had been in constant-hurry mode, until minutes ago when he was forced yet again to stand and not stride on another moving walkway.

Habit, if not addiction, kicked in and he reached for his phone in his pocket. Panic rose when it wasn't there. As he began to flounder around, the sight of the person's backpack blocking his way jogged his memory. He had quickly stuffed his phone into his own backpack when he was at the security gate. Jon yanked his backpack off and dug through several pockets before he found where he had mindlessly stuffed it in his state of hurry. He thumbed it open.

And what he read had moved him from anger to worry to sheer panic.

Jon had hit reply-all when he made the snide Pointy-Haired Boss comment that he had intended only for his coworker Alec. The slow realization that the message went to the entire team, including the Pointy-Haired Boss himself, sent his body into an emotional and physiological whirlwind. The flood of messages from coworkers were ranging from hysterically laughing emojis to one-sentence questions and statements pointing out the now-obvious situation: "Did you know you hit reply-all?"

The text from Alec simply read, "Houston, we have a problem. Call me."

And none of the respondents had hit reply-all in their messages to Jon.

"What did I do? What did I do? What did I do?" Jon's mind immediately began reeling with possible explanations and excuses: "Of course I knew I hit reply-all. It was a joke. Don't we all love *Dilbert?*" Or maybe he would claim that someone had hacked his email and sent this to make him look bad, knowing he was the team member next in line for a promotion.

His gut ached. His could feel his heart pounding in his chest. His neck tightened. His palms were sweating.

All of the frustrations of the entire morning flooded together to the point where Jon was momentarily frozen. Then he heard the looping recording, "The moving walkway is coming to an end. Please watch your step." And it jarred him back to reality. His anger once again took center stage.

Jon knew he had to get on the plane immediately and craft an email that would put everything right. He hoped.

In the panic that had overwhelmed him for the last few minutes, Jon had forgotten that he was late to his gate. Until now. As he looked up at the gate monitor, he realized that he had missed his early boarding spot, the second group was loading, and they were now lining up the final group. He hated not being one of the first passengers on the plane, free to pick the best seat with the best luggage-storage area. That seemed slightly less important at the moment. He only wanted to get on the plane and have time to blame something or somebody else for this mess.

Buddy could get on the plane anytime he wanted. And at six-foot-two and 200 pounds, he enjoyed extra legroom as much as the next person, although he did admit that finding the so-called extra legroom was a diminishing luxury in air travel. On this fine morning, Buddy had gotten caught up in his own reflections on backpacks and their emotional contents, so he had not jumped up when his boarding group was called.

The angry young man that had caught his attention was now frantically digging though his own backpack. Buddy saw the relief on his face when he pulled a phone out. Then he saw the relief turn to panic, then turn to anger. Buddy had seen such an emotional hijack many times. Sometimes a person's body reacts as if it's in a life-or-death situation when it isn't. That often causes what Buddy calls the porcupine response: Everything about the person's face and body screams, "Stay away from me or I will hurt you!"

It was time to board the plane.

Buddy grabbed his backpack.

Chapter 14

"I hate gate lice," were the first words Buddy heard Jon utter as their paths intersected in the awkward flow toward the gate agent. Buddy frowned at the term. He knew that "gate lice" was the derogatory nickname that some sky warriors used to describe anxious travelers who crowded around the gate before their group was called, hoping to claim ever-diminishing overhead bin space before others in their group. Even though he didn't like the term, Buddy was fully aware of how the human traffic jam they created made boarding more difficult. It was another scenario where people were unaware of their backpacks. Boarding passengers struggled to maneuver around large bags and bulky backpacks that were blocking the way.

And many of those doing the blocking didn't even realize it. Or worse, they didn't care.

Buddy shook his head. This was another situation that people stressed about because they didn't fully understand stress. Stress at its core was a physiological and neurological response to a life-threatening situation. You see a poisonous snake, your brain and body take over and tell you to run! Fast! But humans had developed the unique ability in the animal kingdom to stress out about non-life-threatening situations; even worse, humans stay in a state of stress, allowing those lifesaving neurochemicals that were intended for short-term survival, like escaping from the snake, to surge through their body continually. That is when stress is bad for you, Buddy thought. When a person gets and stays stressed about things they shouldn't be stressed about to begin with.

He thought back to the parable about the rattlesnake and the hiker. "You knew what I was when you picked me up."

Jon looked up to see Buddy as they both moved toward the gate agent. Buddy could see Jon's hesitation to push in front of him while at the same time doing just that. With a disarming smile, Buddy said, "Go right ahead. I don't think this plane is leaving without either one of us. And I'm hopeful that we will both land at the same time."

Buddy had used this sentiment many times at many gates. Sometimes the passenger he was letting in front of him smiled back and relaxed at the comment. Some thanked him and moved ahead. Others just stared with a surprised expression that a stranger was actually talking to them. Still others ignored him. Jon seemed to exhibit a mixture of surprise, confusion, and annoyance at Buddy.

Again, Buddy didn't really care too much about how others responded. He was going to be friendly, no matter what. He cared even less about what others thought about him, as long as he was doing the right thing.

This was another fact of life for Buddy:

- ◆ Do the right thing regardless of how others respond.
- ◆ Don't try to make everyone happy. If you do, you'll make yourself miserable.
- ◆ Know that *not* everybody is going to love you, much less like you.

Okay, it was a long fact. But the foundation of it was this: "Do not live your life worried about what other people think of you—or your old leather backpack," Buddy thought with a smile.

Buddy recalled a book he read about common, every-day people who were millionaires, but no one would guess as much. These folks really didn't care about what others thought about them or the stuff they had. If their 12-year-old truck still ran, why on earth did they need a new one? Heck, if their 12-year-old toaster did what a toaster was supposed to do, why did they need a new one?

It was a similar principle with relationships. At least in Buddy's world. If you had the opportunity to be nice to someone—to hold a door, put their large bag into an overhead bin, or say a kind word, why on earth would you not do it? Why care what others think about you for being nice?

Buddy had long ago stopped collecting research articles on the power and importance of simply being nice to others. The research was overwhelming. It was finally showing up in the popular leadership journals. Being nice was always a choice. And it was always the right thing to do. It was even the way to greatly increase your effectiveness as a leader. And the argument about what to do with people who were trying to hurt you or take advantage of you was moot. That was a Chukar chase. It got you chasing after multiple topics like a hunting dog tracking a wily upland game bird. It took you down dead-end trails and rationalizations away from the main subject.

This is not about accepting abuse and hurtful behavior from others. You don't do that. Period. This is about getting out of your own world and being nice to other people regard-less of what people may think of you for doing so. Fact of life.

To Buddy, it went without saying that not caring what others think about you had to first be built on a foundation of personal integrity, strong moral character, and genuine love and care for your fellow travelers on the mothership Earth. If you have an attitude that says, "I don't care what others think about me," but in reality you're a selfish, self-centered jerk, you have some work to do. But if you're a confident, secure, and grounded individual, living life with a goal of leaving the world a better place than you found it, then loving your neighbor should simply be a way of life, regardless of what they give back.

Knowing and living out your own personal core values were the key.

And one of Buddy's core values was to help others along life's journey.

Obviously, at least to those who were paying attention, the man in front of Buddy was a person who was not enjoying the journey on this day. And Buddy was reasonably sure the man wasn't even aware of how much his face and body were broadcasting that fact.

Stressed and angry people don't typically manage their faces very well.

Buddy knew the next few minutes would determine where the conversation was going to go, if it was to go anywhere at all. He was well aware that intervening with angry people was risky. He also knew it was a huge mistake to tell someone they were, or even looked, angry. That's spurring the bull while he's still in the chute.

But you can empathetically connect with another person if you're paying attention—and you try.

Being nice was the best approach.

"Excuse me, son. I couldn't help but notice that you look a little preoccupied? Even bothered? I certainly don't mean to pry, but is everything okay? Anything I can do to help?"

No accusations, no judgments, only observations, followed by an offer. Something easily dismissed by the hearer, yet always—okay, nearly always—made them aware of how they were coming across. Buddy had also learned that if you string the question out, asking several related questions in a row, you give the person a little more time to think about the query and how they might respond.

They all continued to shuffle toward the ticket agent.

Jon did not take advantage of the extra time to think about his words.

He glanced at the tall, boot-wearing gentleman with a denim shirt and a leather backpack slung over his shoulder. Jon's immediate response was, "Well, cowboy, if you can turn back time, great; if not, then I reckon you can't be any help to me at all." The "reckon" was a not-so-subtle, sarcastic shot at Buddy's apparent roots.

Jon started to say, "So you can just save your offer to help for someone who gives a crap," when he looked at Buddy's face for the first time. What he saw caused Jon to pause mid-sentence. The smile was disarming, and the eyes were kind.

Jon changed course and found himself involuntarily taking a deep breath. "Let's just say that in the two and a half hours that I've been awake and getting ready for this incredibly important trip, not one single thing has gone right. It's been a disaster ever since my alarm failed to go off."

Jon knew his words were exaggerated and not completely true. The whole alarm debacle was his fault. He was, consciously or not, attempting to make himself look more like a victim of circumstance amidst the frustrating morning. Even to an absolute stranger. And he wasn't about to tell a stranger about the email fiasco.

Buddy also knew Jon exaggerated. The fact that the young man was standing here about to get on his flight was proof that some things had actually gone right today. The difference between pessimism and optimism is about 180 degrees. The situation hasn't changed; the only difference is how you look at it.

"Well, young man," Buddy said warmly, "I'd wager things are going to go up from here!" Again, Buddy had learned the hard way what not to say. At one time in his life he would have replied, "Hey, idiot, you're getting on a frigging plane, on time. Let's get some perspective here!" That might have been the truth but would not have been helpful. Buddy stayed focused on the positive.

"As a matter of fact," Buddy continued, "I'm even betting this is going to end up being a fantastic day for both of us."

Buddy continued to smile, with his thumb hooked comfortably on his well-adjusted backpack.

Jon was stumped about what to say next. He scanned his boarding pass and headed into the Jetway, still trying to adjust his very uncomfortable backpack.

Chapter 15

Sofia stationed herself in the front galley by the boarding door. With Cecelia still pouting from the rebuke and Collin still dazed by the encounter, Sofia chose to be the first crew member to greet the boarding passengers. In spite of her introverted nature, she knew she would bring energy and enthusiasm to the role. Beyond that, she enjoyed the opportunity to welcome each and every person as they boarded the plane. This included offering a reassuring smile to the obviously nervous flyers, providing excited children a chance to stick their heads in the cockpit and meet the captain, and helping those who struggled to make the 90-degree turn into the narrow aisle because they were dragging their baggage, which seemed to grow larger by the trip. And she had learned to be careful not to get sideswiped by people's backpacks as they made the turn.

About halfway into the boarding process, Sofia's smile grew even larger. Buddy! As an introvert, Sofia loved seeing familiar faces, which was not unusual if you flew the same routes from the same home base often enough. To be honest, what she really loved was seeing those specific frequent flyers who, no matter what, were wearing smiles and choosing to "enjoy the ride." That was one of Buddy's many adages about the journey of life. Folks like Buddy, who understood and embraced the ups and downs of air travel, were always a bonus to have on board.

Sofia remembered one particular trip where their plane was late because of weather conditions. Passengers who were worried about missing their connections were eager to get off as soon as the plane arrived at the gate. When everyone stood to exit, one particular passenger began angrily pushing his way toward the front and was becoming verbally abusive to other passengers when they wouldn't—or couldn't—get out of his way. The crew members were stuck at both ends of the plane and Sofia watched from the front, ready to get on the PA system to ask for calm. Then, Buddy intervened. Sofia wasn't exactly sure what Buddy had said or done, but from her position, it looked like a combination of compassion and directness, kindness and truth. Whatever it was, surrounding passengers smiled and the upset passenger stopped yelling and pushing. He still wasn't happy, but he was waiting his turn.

When Sofia asked Buddy later what he had told the man, Buddy simply grinned and said, "Oh, I just reminded him of a few facts of life. I find that most people need to be reminded of the right thing to do more than be told." She still wondered about his exact words. Buddy had an incredibly kind face; but he also had a very commanding presence. He could light up a room—or a plane—with his energy and expressiveness, both of which were contagious and drew people to him.

But he would also use that charisma to have a tough conversation about the facts of life with someone.

And it didn't hurt that amidst a full shock of gray hair, Buddy looked like he could still wrestle a wild bull to the ground. Which Sofia knew was something he had in fact done.

It was good to see Buddy's familiar, kind face. He had once shared with her his belief that with some hard but rewarding work on ourselves, we all can develop a "yes face," a look that simply tells others, without a word, that you're willing to help them. People can, and should, practice smiling, practice showing enthusiasm, and practice having a "yes face." Buddy had also told her that he was living proof. It was difficult for Sofia to believe it when Buddy told her he used to have "no face" that would, in Buddy's words, "make a train take a dirt road."

Then Sofia noticed that the passenger directly in front of Buddy was indeed wearing a "take a dirt road" face.

"Buddy!" Sofia exclaimed as she moved past Jon to give Buddy a big hug around the neck. "Well, hello, Miss Sofia! Allow me to say that my day has just been made! I was wondering if you'd be on this flight." Buddy was well aware that Sofia was married—he had even met Scott once at the airport. Calling her "Miss Sofia" was just part of who Buddy was.

The boarding line was at a standstill, and Buddy and Sofia were glad to have the chance to chat. "I got to the gate a few minutes later than normal so didn't get to see the crew get on."

"You? Late?" Sofia asked in surprise.

Buddy replied, "Well, I stopped to do some reflecting along my journey here. You know, taking time—"

"To enjoy the ride," Sofia finished his sentence.

Buddy grinned. "And part of that enjoyment is taking time to learn."

The people ahead of them in the aisle struggled to get their bags and backpacks in place. Buddy knew the folks still standing behind him could see that the people in front of them weren't moving. He was very conscious of not standing still, blocking the way of the other travelers anxious to get on board. Buddy was also conscious of where his backpack was, so he wasn't whacking passengers behind him—or Sofia.

As the line started to move, Buddy said, "Stop by and see me sometime. I'll be easy to find."

It was going to be at least a three-and-a-half-hour flight, so Buddy knew Sofia would have a chance to stop by a couple of times for a chat. It wasn't like the quick, 30-minute trip from Austin to Dallas, where flight attendants barely had time to prepare passengers for takeoff and landing. She would also be able to add to the conversation that Buddy had decided he was going to have with the young man who was now hitting about every third portside-aisle passenger with his backpack, completely unaware he was doing it. Buddy was determined to find a seat next to him.

Backpacks are like self-awareness, Buddy thought again. And this guy was a prime example of what a lack of self-awareness looked like.

Jon was ticked off that he didn't get his usual exit-row seat with extra legroom. He would have preferred an airline that allowed your status to get you first-class upgrades, but his company had changed its travel policy so the lowest fare must be purchased at least two weeks ahead of time whenever possible. Even booking flights was taken out of the hands of the travelers in order to ensure company compliance.

Still, Jon had status on this airline that ensured early boarding—as long as he got there on time.

He wedged into the first completely open row. "At least I get my preferred window seat," Jon grumbled, again not real-izing he was saying it loud enough for anyone paying atten-tion to hear. Which most people weren't. Which Buddy was.

"Not one single thing has gone right, huh?" Buddy thought.

Jon shoved his carry-on in the overhead bin, climbed into his seat, reached over and put the middle seat tray down, put his backpack at his feet and opened it up.

Buddy stepped into the aisle seat in Jon's row.

"Mind if I sit here?" Buddy asked. It wasn't really a ques-tion. He was already sitting down by the time the words were out of his mouth.

Sofia glanced down the aisle and, as she expected, saw Buddy choosing to sit next to the guy who had boarded the plane with him. Sofia thought, "Buddy brought positive energy on board and this guy is sure trying to neutralize it with negativity."

Good thing positivity can win.

Jon half looked up. He didn't quite catch Buddy's question, but he didn't care anyway. He was digging in his backpack as panic again seized his body.

He had been so confident that he had everything he needed. He had told Grace and himself more than once that he knew what was in his backpack. Up until that point, you would have thought Jon's face couldn't have become any more negative. Until now.

Because the laptop was not in his backpack.

Chapter 16

Sofia was going through her atypical preflight announcements, "ginned up," as Buddy called it, by humor. "If you don't like the flight attendants or our humor, there are six ways off of this plane," as they pointed to the exits. She continued, "If you're traveling with more than one child, what on earth were you thinking?" And then she got to a line that still made Buddy smile: "If the oxygen mask pops out, secure your mask first and then decide which child has the most potential."

Buddy had read that a passenger had complained to the CEO of the airline about the jokes made during the FAA-regulated instructions. The passenger thought the safety announcements were "too serious an issue to joke about." The CEO, as the story went, wrote back a simple, four word note: "We will miss you."

This airline was going to stay true to their core value of having fun, regardless of passenger complaints. The CEO didn't even offer the passenger a free drink coupon to give the airline another try. They would be the same airline regardless of whether or not this passenger returned. Buddy knew that knowing your core values and staying true to them, even when others don't like them, is foundational to having strong self-awareness.

Buddy also knew that a good sense of humor, including the rare yet vital ability to laugh at oneself, was paramount to loving life and enjoying the ride. Fact of life.

Right now, Buddy was busy meeting the young man whose face had moved from angry to downright ashen as he was digging feverishly in his backpack.

Buddy had learned that people cuss for a variety of reasons: to fit in, demonstrate hostility toward others, out of habit, or to express anger or surprise at someone or something. He had once heard cussing likened to honking the horn on your car—humans cuss to get someone's attention. Still, social norms usually prevented most people from releasing the chain of words that Buddy just heard from his new neighbor in row 16 in an audience of strangers.

Buddy was also aware that anger and fear were fraternal twins that shared a room in the basement; they were intimately related, had the same roots of origin, and could often be alike in purpose and physiology. Yet, like twins, they looked different to others. And they could act differently, as well. One could be shy and withdrawn while the other was loud and explosive.

Two sides of the same coin was another way to describe these two workhorse emotions. Typically, fear morphed into anger. Tails flipped to heads.

Buddy had just witnessed heads going back to tails.

A few moments ago, Buddy's seatmate was lashing out at everyone and everything, feeling mistreated, singled out, and abused by the world. He was apparently looking for something in his backpack that he believed was going to help him set the world right and vindicate him from the perceived injustices of the day. Now, he seemed to realize that the thing he was looking for wasn't where he had believed it to be. His hot temperament and angry skin had just turned cold. This was actually one of the physiological differences between anger and fear—skin temperature. It was how the twins showed up differently.

Buddy didn't stare; he simply watched.

For one moment, Jon contemplated grabbing his backpack and sprinting off the plane. He could call Grace to bring his laptop to a halfway point between the airport and home and then catch the next flight out. Then Jon closed his eyes, laid his head back against his seat, and let out a deep sigh. He remembered that Grace was out with a client for the day. Doing the quick math in his head, Jon knew he could never make the round-trip between the airport and home and still catch a plane in time for the client meeting.

Jon felt, and Buddy could see, a degree of defeat setting in. Actually, it was much more than a degree, Buddy thought. Jon looked more like he was on the losing team in the bottom of the ninth, with two out and two strikes on the batter.

Without the laptop, which contained the client presentation, the budget spreadsheet, and his notes for both, Jon didn't even think about using his phone to reply to the emails. While getting on the plane, he had convinced himself that this day simply could not get any worse.

He was wrong.

Sofia had finished the announcements and was now walking the aisle, making sure seatbelts were fastened and backpacks were where they were supposed to be. As she approached, Buddy asked, "Ma'am, could you help with this seatbelt thing? You went over that kind of fast."

"Well, sir," Sofia started, "If you look in your seat-back pocket, we have a special instruction sheet for cowboys who haven't been in a vehicle made after 1965. You know, judging from the look of you, it appears that you could use a seatbelt on your horse."

Some passengers muffled a laugh; most were feeling uncomfortable by the conversation. Then all realized that both were smiling and must be friends. It was easy to tell that the old cowboy could laugh at himself with the best of them.

Sofia's presence also caused Jon to open his eyes and look over at the two who obviously did not understand the depths of what he was going through.

"Who's your new friend?" Sofia asked.

"Not sure," Buddy replied. "We haven't been formally introduced . . . yet."

"Buddy, you wouldn't know formal if it hit you on the nose, but I must say, I'm surprised. It usually takes you all of three seconds to introduce yourself and another 30 seconds to find out someone's life story."

"To be honest," Jon muttered, "he started to talk to me while we were getting on the plane. I guess I kind of blew him off."

"That never stopped him before," Sofia replied.

Sofia looked over at Jon. "Sir, I'd like to introduce you to—and warn you about—Buddy Smith. Common, I know. He has a much more formal name but, as I alluded to, I don't think he can even spell *formal*. But I have to tell you, there is not a better buddy on the planet, not to mention on this plane. And you are?"

Buddy was already reaching out to shake Jon's hand as Sofia finished her question. "Jon," he replied, meeting Buddy for one of the firmest handshakes he had ever felt. "And I'm Sofia," Sofia quickly completed the circle, shaking his hand, as well. "And I would love to continue this greet-fest, but I've got to make sure these souls are ready to get this hunk of metal up in the air."

She leaned in, closer to Buddy's ear. "And make sure my cabin crew is choosing to have the right attitude. It didn't start well today."

Sofia stood erect, winked at Buddy, confident she had secured an ally to help with her team, and was about to walk away.

Jon wasn't quite sure what was happening, but he found himself welcoming the distraction. "One question, please?" he asked.

Sofia paused. "Shoot," she said. "Which I realize is not great terminology for plane travel."

Jon halfway smiled. "Why is there not a 'better buddy on the planet' than this gentleman?"

Now Sofia smiled. "Well? Let me put it this way. You've heard of folks that would give you the shirt off their back?" Jon nodded. "This man would give you his shirt, pants, boots, and even his horse, if you needed it. Even more, he will gladly share his extensive, and often cowboy-blunt, wisdom on life and love, especially with those who are struggling. So maybe, just maybe, they won't find themselves in the same predicament again. Maybe it will even help you avoid predicaments like your face tells us you are in right now."

Jon pursed his lips and felt somewhat embarrassed by the callout.

"And even more," Sofia continued, "Buddy helps so you can pay it forward to someone else in need of some kindness."

Sofia winked at Buddy again and could swear she almost saw him blush.

"And he is usually good for a laugh . . . or five. Jon, I'm not sure if you know this or not, but good 'ol belly laughter does amazing, positive things for your brain. It reduces stress hormones, improves your mood, lowers your blood pressure. Heck, it even improves your memory. Yup, we can all always use a good laugh."

She and Buddy both knew that Jon could use one.

Sofia took a step but then stopped to look at them both one more time.

"Even if we're only laughing at ourselves."

Jon thought about what his words and his face must be communicating to people.

"And Mr. Jon," Sofia said as she moved to the next row, "I need you to push your belongings fully under the seat. In case there is an emergency, we can't have anybody tripping over your backpack."

Chapter 17

"I have never met that crazy woman in my life," Buddy started, "so you can ignore whatever it was she was just babbling on about."

"Keep it up, cowboy," Sofia hollered over her shoulder as she moved on down the aisle. "The sky marshals need something to do. And put that middle tray up. The boarding door is closed and you're not fooling anybody!"

Buddy put the tray up, smiled at Jon, and said, "I think we have the row to ourselves." Jon was slightly embarrassed by his ploy, but before he could say anything, Buddy continued, "And I am sure glad to make your acquaintance, Jon."

Jon still wasn't sure that he wanted to get into a conversation at the moment but realizing that Buddy had purposely eased his embarrassment by quickly moving past it, he found himself responding, "Likewise." Plus, the distraction was more than welcomed.

Typically, the first thing Jon did after taking his seat was put on his headphones so he didn't have to speak with anyone, or even listen to anyone, for that matter.

Circumstances of the last few minutes had prevented that this time. And maybe, Jon thought, that was going to be a good thing. Maybe.

"So, what is your formal name?" Jon queried, surprising himself that he was actually taking the lead in this conversation.

"Royce Jefferson Smith," Buddy replied, in as serious a tone as he could muster. "But if you tell anyone, I may have to hog-tie you and stuff you in the cargo hold." Jon still wasn't sure how to take Buddy, but trusting Sofia's words, he replied, "I can see why you go by Buddy."

"Exactly!" Buddy laughed. "Maybe I should have hog-tied my parents for giving me that name!" Now Jon laughed. "*Aww*, I'm just playing," Buddy continued. "My folks were great people. My dad was a hard-working rancher who gave me my work ethic and my dear mom was a schoolteacher who gave me my love of learning. As a matter of fact, after my older sister started calling me Buddy because she couldn't pronounce *brother*, my parents were the ones that decided to make it a permanent nickname. They thought it was a better fit for me, too. I can never thank them enough for all they did for me."

"Sounds like you had an idyllic, perfect family," Jon observed, thinking back about his less-than-perfect family encounters just this morning.

"Idyllic, yes. Perfect? Far from it. That family doesn't exist. That *life* doesn't exist. Heck, that *day* doesn't exist," Buddy said very matter-of-factly. "Which makes me think of your comments back at the gate. And even more when it seemed like something you thought was in your backpack turned out not to be there, right?"

Jon felt his frustrations and his fear returning. Furthermore, he was suddenly agitated by this stranger asking him questions, even if he was trying to be a buddy. "You may be friendly," Jon thought, "but that doesn't solve my problems." He needed to get back into problem-solving mode.

Jon's tone became cold, once again. "Well, sir, I doubt very seriously you want to hear about my day, and I doubt even more that, even in your wisdom, you could do anything to help my situation. I'm in such a fluster right now, that I need to shut down this conversation and . . ." Jon paused and let out a deep sigh.

"And what?" Buddy asked warmly.

Jon stared blankly toward the back of the seat in front of him. "I was going to say, 'and get started on fixing things.' But I'm not even sure where to start. Well, I did know where to start, but that all blew up with the backpack."

"*Hmm*. Can I ask what you were looking for?"

"Crap!" Jon suddenly exclaimed as he remembered the email response he intended to write as soon as he was settled. The absent laptop and seatmate introductions had caused him to forget all about it. They were already taxiing out to the runway, but Jon thought if he hurried, he could still get out a reasonable response from his phone to everyone to explain the Pointy-Haired Boss comment before they took off. Even though this was now Plan B.

He just had to get people to listen to his side of story.

Buddy knew that the best thing at this moment was to not say anything else. It was going to be a long flight and there would be more time to talk and to listen. For now, he waited.

Sofia made her way up the aisle one last time on the way to her jump seat in the front of the plane. As she approached their row, she paused and asked Buddy, "All buckled up, cowboy?" Then, she noticed that Jon was scrolling quickly through his phone, which was, most likely, not in airplane mode. Sofia knew that the concerns of the early 1990s that cell phone interference could cause a crash were now all but moot. But too many people on their phones all searching full blast for a cell signal can cause minor skips in communication signals between pilots and air-traffic controllers, posing an annoyance to those who are working diligently to get passengers to their destinations safely. Plus, for now, keeping phones in airplane mode is the law.

It also made her think about the almost-lost art of listening. Fully listening to someone takes effort. It is a whole-body experience that could be practiced and improved. Listening is actually the most important communication skill because, all by itself, it communicates that you care about the person speaking.

Listening to the pre-flight announcements was a little different, Sofia recognized. She didn't expect people who traveled all of the time to give their undivided attention to the instructions. Even so, on every flight that Sofia had been on lately, someone had to be personally reminded to put their seat upright or tray table up, or do something with their backpack.

It reminded her of a recent flight where oxygen masks did necessarily deploy, only to be put on incorrectly by at least a dozen people.

Sofia thought, "People don't have communication problems. They have listening problems."

"Jon, are you in airplane mode?" Sofia asked.

"Hold on! Hold on!" Jon shot back without ever taking his eyes off his phone. "I've got to get this email out before we take off! I can't tell you how life-and-death this is!"

"Well, Jon? I'm not sure about your email but, for the people on this plane, real life and death is taking off without interference." Sofia knew it was a little dramatic and she realized that most people didn't understand her response was meant to encourage people to be considerate. "Once we get to the magical kingdom above 10,000 feet, we'll have Wi-Fi. You can finish your email then."

Jon looked up angrily and was about to tell Sofia to just leave him the heck alone, when he found himself greeted by not one but two kind faces. Sofia and Buddy were both looking at him intently, yet smiling. Jon found himself drawn once again toward something in these two people—something, Jon was realizing, that he did not have. He took a deep breath.

For the third time in 15 minutes, Jon put his head back in resignation.

He turned off his phone, reached forward, and mindlessly shoved it somewhere in his backpack.

Chapter 18

Buddy used the next few minutes to think about the best way to start the conversation he planned to have with Jon. He had learned—again, the hard way and with coaching from Truman—that in emotionally charged situations, as this obviously was, there were two questions to keep top of mind: one, what do I need to say that is helpful and, two, how do I say it in a manner where the other person can actually hear it? It was all about creating emotional safety. It isn't about knowing the answer before you ask, like lawyers think they can do, or controlling the other person's response, which is impossible. It would be, once more, acting with other people's best interest in mind by making it safe for them to connect with him.

Even if they're not sure what their best interest is.

Google had even recently announced that emotional safety was a key to healthy, highly effective teams.

Buddy knew this was goal number one. Even without Googling it.

He also knew that it was well demonstrated in relationship research that arguments end how they begin and that a vital skill for managing conflict well was to avoid "harsh startups."[1] If a fight started with yelling and hot emotions, it would end with yelling and hot emotions. If a fight started with accusations and finger-pointing, it would end with accusations and finger-pointing—or worse. The lack of safety created by harsh words puts people in a defensive, flight-or-fight mode.

The old "sticks and stones" adage is stupid.

Fact of life: Words matter.

Before the 10,000-feet mark Buddy calmly said, "Jon, I am terribly sorry that this has been such a rough morning for you. Do you want to finish telling me about what wasn't in your backpack?"

In his younger days, Buddy's questions would have gone straight to "why" this email was life or death, and then quickly pointed out that unless the email was to an organ donor or a hit man, it most likely was not life or death. He would still get to that point, but in a more roundabout way. He wasn't trying to avoid the conflict; he simply didn't want to escalate it. Now Buddy had started with empathy, a previously unanswered question, and a word choice that said that he simply wanted to continue a conversation.

Empathy, emotional safety, and freedom for the other to respond—or not.

"My laptop," Jon stated stoically. "And before you start asking about whether the files are 'backed up to the cloud,' or, 'Why can't someone send you what you need?' and on and on, let me jump to the end and say it was a brand-new laptop and our IT department hasn't yet connected me to the company cloud. I wanted to have it for this presentation I'm giving, so I made IT give it to me yesterday before they had configured it. Last night I created a new presentation from scratch. It exists only on that laptop. I must have left it under the edge of my bed where I put it after finishing up last night."

Jon sighed deeply and continued. "And, if you must know, all of my newly typed client notes are on it. As well as the spreadsheet I promised to finish for my boss while I was on this flight. And, to top it all off, my wife chose today to meet with one of her clients, whose office is a good two-hour drive from our home, so she's not there to send me anything. Which wouldn't really matter, anyway, since all I have is this phone, which won't run the presentation. And I am *not* going to look so unprofessional as to ask my client to use one of their computers."

He continued to stare blankly into space. He thought about how he wanted the laptop to properly return his boss's email. He had planned to bury his excuse for the PHB comment by sending the completed spreadsheet along with it. The attempt to use the phone for the reply a few minutes ago was Plan B. He wanted to address at least one of his life-threatening problems.

Jon looked down at his backpack. "And now that I think about it, I not only boasted to my boss about having that spreadsheet done, I also bragged to all of the other directors in the department, trying to prove that I'm more on top of things than they are." Another sigh. "That email . . . that email is going to cost me dearly."

He now looked straight at Buddy for the first time. "So, my wise new buddy. Any words of wisdom for me on this? Any precious gems that are going to save my can in this mess?"

"*Hmm*," Buddy intoned.

"I didn't think so," Jon quietly said, as he looked back down at his backpack. "That thing sure has caused me a lot of problems today," as he gave it a little kick.

Buddy had been intently listening and patiently waiting for his moment to jump back into the conversation. He couldn't have planned a better opening.

"What thing is that?" Buddy asked. "Your backpack?"

"Yes, my backpack," Jon continued. Buddy could tell that Jon wanted to keep talking, so he remained silent. Often, people who are struggling to sort out an array of emotions will keep talking as they are trying to make sense of what they are feeling. The human brain has an amazing will to survive and make sense of what is happening both in and around it. People often need help with connecting the dots and Buddy knew his time for that would come. That was something else he had learned from Dr. T.

"I started my day by tripping over it. Actually, it started with the alarm not going off as planned and then stepping on a deadly dog toy; after that, I crashed into my backpack in the middle of my closet. My wife had actually put it there so I would know where it was." Jon closed his eyes and laid his head back, almost in regret. "And then I even leveled my four-year-old with the darn thing as I was heading through the bedroom door."

Buddy smiled at the "deadly dog toy" remark and was happy to hear Jon adding a dose of humor to his story, even if there was blaming sarcasm behind it.

"*Hmm.*" Buddy said again. "Sounds like your wife is very thoughtful and tries to look out for you."

"Grace? Yeah. She's great." Jon paused, then his face grew a little stern once again. "Though she did make me mad by nagging me about whether or not I had everything I needed in my backpack." *Humph.* "I guess I was wrong to snap at her for that, especially considering that I did not have what I thought I had in my backpack."

Buddy thought that was a good step number two. It showed Jon was starting to take personal responsibility, though he still had a long way to go.

It was time to start directing the conversation. Keeping it safe does not mean avoiding the conflict. It simply means that people don't feel judged or maligned for their thoughts, opinions, or simply who they are. It means that there is enough relational capacity created through caring to allow for healthy conflict.

"Jon, can I tell you something that I learned today about backpacks?"

Chapter 19

"See that young lady a few rows ahead with the red head-phones on?" Buddy asked, nodding in her direction. "When she got on the plane, she was carrying the very definition of an over-stuffed backpack. Her arms were through both straps so it was dead in the middle of her back. She couldn't see it unless she had a big mirror or a selfie-stick or an owl's head," Buddy laughed.

"And?" Jon asked.

"And, she hit almost every aisle passenger between the front of the plane and her seat there in row 13," Buddy stated. "Then, as she was stuffing her phone and headphones in the seat pocket and then trying to get her purse under the seat, she almost took the head off of the guy across the aisle."

Buddy continued to laugh. "And it was Groundhog's Day until the gentleman put his hand up in self-defense to keep from getting whacked the same way over and over. Reminded me of a bull in a chute, banging everything around it. Except the bull is aware of exactly what he's doing and whom he's whacking."

"So, she's a selfish jerk," Jon observed.

"*Hmm.* No, I don't think so," Buddy replied. "And let me highlight something very important: I am *not* judging people. I'll leave that to the courts. Our judgments of why people behave the way they do are wrong more often than not."

Jon thought back about the military family in the terminal. And his conversation with Grace about the fundamental attribution error. Buddy was right about being wrong. And it put an ache in his gut.

"No, sir," Buddy continued, "this is about observing behaviors. And as I observe her, she has a kind and pleasant demeanor. She smiles. And has remorse and apologizes. The man must have finally said something to her because she turned around and said, 'I'm so sorry; I don't fly much.' I could hear her from here. And when she turned to apologize, she whacked that other guy in the seat in front of her!" Buddy laughed again.

"No, the issue isn't being selfish; the issue is being completely unaware. Completely unaware of her backpack."

"Okay, if she's not a selfish jerk," Jon found himself mentally retreating from his harsher judgment, "she must be completely clueless about the ways of life."

Buddy cocked his head back and looked straight at Jon, and with boldness yet kindness in his voice, he asked, "Well, Jon, are you 'completely clueless about the ways of life'?"

"What?!? You gotta be . . . Me?!?" Jon stammered. "No! Hey, just because I sometimes lose my cool or get frustrated with people, doesn't make me clueless, or a selfish jerk! Everybody gets mad and lets their frustrations get the best of them at times. And I certainly didn't smack everybody with my backpack when I was coming down the aisle."

"*Hmm*," Buddy began.

The "*Hmm*" was beginning to bother Jon. He was starting to understand he was about to be told he was wrong. "I agree you didn't smack everybody; it was more like every other person on that side of the plane," Buddy pointed out, nodding his head.

"No, I didn't," Jon started to protest.

"I'd be happy to confirm with some of them," Buddy stated with a smile.

"No . . . no," Jon replied. He realized he had been in such a hurry to get in his seat and get out his laptop that he wasn't sure what had happened as he came down the aisle. "I didn't think I hit anyone," Jon said in a quieter, more doubtful tone.

"About that thing I realized today," Buddy began.

Jon somewhat reluctantly continued to listen.

"As a business leader," Buddy flattered, "I'm sure you've heard of the importance of self-awareness."

"Sure," Jon started. "Leaders need to understand their personalities and be aware of their strengths and their weaknesses. It's being aware of who you are." Jon thought Buddy would be impressed with his quick and accurate definition.

Instead he got the "*Hmm.*"

Jon prepared.

"That's a start," Buddy continued, "That is certainly part of self-awareness, but there is so much more." Buddy had a way of giving a compliment while at the same time letting a person know they're wrong.

"What I thought of today is that self-awareness is like a backpack."

"Like a backpack?" Jon questioned.

"Like a backpack," Buddy continued. "And, as I've reflected on it, I've realized that there are four things we need to know or do when it comes to our backpack—not someone else's backpack. *Our* backpack."

"And?" Jon genuinely inquired.

"One, we need to know exactly which one is ours, decide what we want in it, and accept it. Two, we must take responsibility for it . . . all of it . . . at all times. Three, we need to understand exactly how it impacts anybody and everybody around us." Buddy paused.

"And?" Jon asked.

"Let's start with those three. We'll get to number four quick enough."

"Well, okay," Jon grinned, "at least I had part of it . . . I am guessing my definition would fall somewhere within number one?"

"That's right!" Buddy continued, "And thanks for paying attention!"

"Oh, believe me, I'm paying attention. And as you describe those three components, it doesn't sound that hard. I think most people—except maybe the young lady up there—are pretty good at being self-aware. Granted, we all have bad days when we whack a few people, like I did, but if you ask the average person, I'm betting they would say they do those three well. What do you think about that, Buddy?"

"*Hmmmm.*" A little more drawn out than normal, Jon noticed.

"To be honest, Jon, when it comes to full self-awareness, it's almost as rare as hen's teeth. Honestly, I think most folks are *big hat, no cattle.*"

"Okay," Jon joined in. "I'll bite. What does 'big hat, no cattle' mean?"

"Oh, that's how you describe someone pretending to be something they're not. Like a person trying to be a cowboy simply by dressing up like one. They're trying to look the part but in reality they wouldn't know a steer from a bull."

Buddy cocked his head and looked toward Jon. "It's the same with self-awareness. One report I read surmised that while 95 percent of people think they are self-aware, in reality, only 10 to 15 percent of them actually are.[1] I don't know if those numbers are exact, but I'd bet they're pretty close. In other words, *big hat, no cattle.*"

Jon sat in silence.

"And what makes that statistic worrisome," Buddy continued, "Is that full self-awareness is the key to living a successful life, both at home and at work.

"Again, this is not about judging people. We've all been clueless at times. Heck, we've all been selfish jerks at times. But we all can grow. We all need to grow.

"Jon, can I be straight-up honest with you?" Buddy asked boldly.

Jon nodded his head without even thinking about it.

"I believe that most of the problems you have had today stem from *underutilized self-awareness*." Buddy knew that was a little softer than *lack of self-awareness*, though they are the same thing. Still, underutilized implies that growth can occur.

Jon still sat in silence.

"And believe me, son," Buddy continued, "I've certainly had plenty of days like that, too. Yes, we can all grow into our big hats a little bit better. And we first do that by understanding, and taking full responsibility for, our backpacks."

Chapter 20

Buddy glanced up toward the galley and noticed Sofia in a deep conversation with another crew member. Apparently, someone was not happy, and that someone was not Sofia. Based on the depth of Buddy's friendship with Sofia, he presumed that she would handle the situation with professionalism and kindness.

Buddy knew Sofia's core values. Her true core values. Not the overstated, undervalued, often-ignored type of values that decorate many corporate lobbies and company letterheads around the globe.

Sofia's values were not only well thought out, they were also well lived out.

As Buddy had studied people and organizations, he'd come to believe that core values should not be a simple, boilerplate list of words, like *integrity, teamwork,* and *honesty.* No one should be in business if they don't believe in and live out integrity, teamwork, and honesty, as well as many other basic values. Buddy remembered one speaker he heard describing those as simply "permission to play"[1] values. Those were table-stakes that got you in the game.

If you choose to have a written core value, Buddy believed you should write it with a definition that made it clear and real to everyone who reads it. A core value needs to connect with people's heads and their hearts. It needs to be unique to the individual or the company.

Core values should be something that are distinctively focused on what makes us *us*. And, just as important, they are what will help guide us. They help us know what to say yes to and what so say no to. Core values should take what may be a more common, table-stakes word, and drive it clearly home while aligning it with our mission; it connects to our reason for existing.

For example, one company in his home state had chosen *integrity* as the top core value. But it was fine-tuned so it wouldn't seem generic. *Integrity* was followed by something that tied it to the mission of the company: "Integrity: Closing the gap between our public and private selves."

That was good. And it described what this company did in the leadership development space.

It was the same with Sofia.

Buddy knew that one of Sofia's values was *kindness*, but she had written it down as, "Be kind, because kindness matters to every person you meet."

Integrity was now living out that value. Everyday. With everybody. Always.

Integrity was one of Buddy's favorite words. Not because it was a common core value, but because he knew its origin—its true meaning.

Linguistically, *integrity* is rooted in *integer,* meaning *intact,* or, in math, *whole*. At its core, to be a person of integrity meant you were the same person everywhere you went. Buddy would shake his head when he would see a news story where a powerful figure had been disgraced due to bad choices in their personal lives, but publicly declare, "I have always been a person of integrity in my professional life."

Can't do it. That's not integrity. You gotta close the gap.

He thought of one company that had the word *integrity* splattered across their annual report to their investors. And they were simultaneously lying to those investors, as well as their employees and the FCC. That didn't end well. And it wasn't integrity.

If you're a jerk, then have "being a jerk" as a core value and be the same jerk everywhere you go. That would show more integrity than that company.

Core values: Know 'em. Own 'em. Live 'em.

He knew Sofia would be strong but kind—even if the other person wasn't.

Because if it is truly a core value, you live it out, even when—especially when—it is difficult to do so.

As Buddy was temporarily lost in thought about Sofia, Jon pulled him back. Ten minutes ago, he would have declared he was self-aware; like the 95 percent of people who would say the same thing. Now, he wondered if he was actually in the 85 percent who were not.

"Okay, Buddy, I don't want to be 'big hat, no cattle.' When it comes to self-awareness, I want to be an expert on bulls and steers and momma heifers," he ended with a grin.

Jon thought he might impress Buddy by throwing in another cow word.

It didn't work.

Buddy smiled back. "Well, Jon, I will be delighted to continue this conversation about the culture of bovines, but let's start with the understanding that what makes a heifer a heifer is the fact that she has not yet been a momma."

"Big hat, no cattle, huh?" Jon blushed.

"That's alright, Jon, because you just stated the most important part of this journey. You want to be an expert, which I assume means you want to learn and you to want to change, correct?"

"Yes, sir," Jon quickly moved past his embarrassment. "Especially if being an expert in self-awareness is the key to success at work."

"Well, sir," Buddy continued, "to use a cowboy term that I am sure you do know the meaning of, you need to 'hold your horses' a minute."

Now they both smiled.

"I didn't say anything about being an expert," Buddy continued. "That's impossible."

"Really?" Jon said, surprised.

"Oh, someone may become a subject-matter expert on self-awareness, but no one has perfect self-awareness."

"Really?" Jon asked again. "Why not?"

"The first reason is that we all, as we've said, will have a bad day. We have all been on the stressed-out ledge of life and let our emotions get the better of us. That doesn't mean we aren't still responsible for our emotions and our bad choices. Frankly, the more we grow in self-awareness, the more good choices we make and the fewer bad choices we make. Still, fact of life: We all make emotional mistakes."

"Okay," Jon replied, still focused on every word and remembering that Buddy had said that the bulk of his problems on this day were due to his *underutilized self-awareness*. "And the second reason?"

"Because of another fact of life: No matter how well we know each other, you don't fully know what it's like to be me, and I don't fully know what it's like for you to be *with* me. And vice-versa." Buddy let that sink in. "You don't know what it's like to be me," Buddy repeated.

And Jon finished, "And I don't fully know what it's like to be *with* me."

They again both sat quietly in the drone of the engines. Jon thought back through his whole morning of judging people. It was more than misjudging the mom and kids going to meet their father.

It was the police officer on the side of the road.

The driver in front of him.

The attendant at valet parking.

It was all of the people in the security line.

It was even Grace, when all she was trying to do was help him.

Buddy interrupted his thoughts.

"Jon, it begins with a willingness to be on the journey of growth, a journey to understand our backpacks, what we want in them, and what we may need to take out of them."

"What we want in them or out of them?" Jon questioned.

"Like what core values do we want in them, to guide us, especially on rough days like you're having today, and what behaviors do we want out of them, like ones that are hurtful to others."

Buddy let that sink in, too.

"I'm there," Jon said enthusiastically. "I want to take the journey. Maybe it can help me improve things at work."

"Oh, it sure as heck will, but can I tell you another thing that I think will mean a lot to you?"

Jon nodded.

"I didn't say this was only about success at work. Full self-awareness is also the key to great friendships and the family we all want to have. On this journey, we become better mates, parents, partners, and friends, as we become better at, well, understanding our backpacks."

Chapter 21

"Okay, Buddy. Let's rock and roll! You said that first of all we need to know which backpack is ours, decide what we want in it, and . . .?"

"Accept it," Buddy filled in.

"Okay. I'm not sure I get that last one, Buddy." Jon said. "I thought this was about taking a journey of improvement. And doesn't deciding to improve something imply that I am not accepting things the way they are?"

"That is a great question, Jon! I love the way you are thinking about your backpack. But, if you don't mind, I'd like to take the points in order; then the idea of accepting our backpacks will make more sense. That okay with you?"

"You're the boss," Jon replied.

Buddy laughed. "Son, the only thing I'm boss of is me and my backpack, and there are times that I should be fired from that job. But 'boss' is a good place to start.

"Think about the best boss you ever had, Jon." Buddy paused to let Jon reflect. "You got 'em?"

"I do."

"Okay, tell me about 'em."

"Her name was Vera. She owned the neighborhood grocery store where I worked during high school. Man, was she a hard worker. And smart. Did she know the grocery business! Wow."

"All good traits," Buddy said, "but what made Vera the *best* boss you ever had? I'm guessing you've had some other bosses with some if not all of those traits."

Jon paused and thought.

"Yeah, you're right about that," Jon continued.

"She made things fun. Even though she was extremely confident, she could laugh at herself when she made mistakes. I always loved that about her."

Buddy nodded and continued to listen.

"She was always challenging us to improve ourselves, but she was equally good at encouraging us to learn what made us unique.

"You know, Buddy, I guess what made her so great was that I knew she cared about me for who I was. She challenged me to grow and work hard, but I didn't think she was ever trying to change me *as a person*. She'd ask about my family, what I wanted to do after high school, how I was doing in school. Things like that. And—"

"And what?" Buddy pushed.

"At her core, she was a very principled person. She would talk to me about how important it was to identify those things that we valued most and then to live by those values every day."

"And do you think that she just stumbled across those values? Like tripping over a backpack?" Buddy asked with a grin.

"No," Jon said thoughtfully, "She had obviously decided that those were things that were important to her." He continued to reflect. "Now that you ask about her, I remember something that she used to say all the time. It had been very important to me as I was starting college—and even when I was deciding to marry Grace."

"And what was that?"

"Wisdom is knowing the right thing to do. Integrity is doing it."

Buddy simply smiled. "She was a very wise woman, indeed," Buddy responded.

"Oh, she was," Jon replied. "She most definitely was."

"This conversation reminds me of another great saying."

"What's that?" Jon queried.

"People don't need tellin' near as much as they need remindin'."

Jon thought about that.

"Jon, when we think of the people that we admire and reflect on what makes them endearing to us, it always comes back to the fact that they are confident people who know themselves well. And, just as important, they are principled people who behave in a way that demonstrates that they care for us.

"Coaches, teachers, youth leaders, bosses, whoever. The ones we admire listened to us, encouraged us, believed in us, challenged us, taught us, respected us, and, ultimately, they loved us well. They helped us, so to speak, with our backpacks.

"And they were the same people everywhere they went. Work, home, with the server at the restaurant or with—"

"The flight attendant," Jon finished.

Buddy continued to smile.

"Before we were knee-high to a hound dog we were all taught by parents, teachers, faith-leaders, and others about the importance of caring for our neighbors. Of being kind to others. As adults, we get so dang busy that we speed through life with horse-blinders on and forget those lessons.

"As such, we often need a remindin'.

"Jon, without knowing it, or maybe you're starting to realize it, when you described Vera, you covered everything in the first part about our backpacks."

"I did?"

"Yes, sir, you did! Self-awareness begins with knowing which backpack is ours. That, as you said, means knowing everything we can about our personality, what makes us tick, our strengths, those things we are good at and give us energy, as well as those things we are not so good at. It is a lifelong journey of learning what makes us *us*."

"*Sooo*," Jon interrupted. "I may not know cattle, but I got that part right." Jon grinned.

Buddy grinned, too. "Then we need to clearly identify the values we want in our backpacks, decide to put them in there, and then live by them. Like your boss, Vera. And like Miss Sofia up there, who I know has chosen as one of her core values, 'Be kind, because kindness matters to every person you meet.'"

Buddy continued, "We decide what's important to us, our values, and put those in our backpack first. And we remind ourselves of those values daily.

"Our values help us make decisions; as I said, they help us know what to say yes to and what to say no to. They are a guide to a meaningful life because we are guided by principles that are meaningful to us!"

"I know companies and organizations spend a lot of time crafting value statements," Jon commented. "They don't always spend much time reminding people what they are or evaluating things by those values."

"Agreed," Buddy said. "Leaders spend a lot of time creating what some have called aspirational values. Those things they think they want or need to be. They choose *teamwork* because that's how they want their employees to work, but, in reality, the company structure promotes individualism, so people are confused.

"Core values have to be who we are, so much so that if and when we violate them, it bothers us, and we correct our behavior. And to remind ourselves of our core values, it helps to write them down."

Jon reflected on that. "I've never thought a lot about how individuals should take the time to clearly define their own values. But I can see how that's important. That is, if you choose to truthfully live by them, like Vera.

"But I'm not sure why someone like Vera would have had to write them down," Jon continued. "I mean, do you really need to write down 'be kind to others' to remember to do it?"

"Well, Jon? What do you think?" Buddy paused. "How many people have you not been nice to this morning alone?"

"Touché," Jon said, blushing.

"So, my friend," Buddy continued, "as wiser folks have said, 'First things first.' Whatever core value exercise or questionnaire you want to use is completely up to you. Again, you probably know your values. You just need remindin'. That's why it's good to write them down—and make sure they are meaningful, memorable, and actionable phrases. And remind yourself of them every single day. Like 'be nice to everybody. Always.'"

"Got it." Jon said. "I will know which backpack is mine by understanding everything I can about me, my personality, and my strengths. Then I will decide what I want in my backpack to guide me by clearly defining my core values—and reminding myself of them, correct?"

"Square on the nose!" Buddy replied.

"But I am still lost on what it means to 'accept my own backpack.'"

Chapter 22

Cecelia was making her way down the aisle, pad and pen in hand. She didn't appear any more joyful or warm than when Buddy saw her earlier. She still appeared annoyed at, well, everything. She started taking orders at the row in front of Buddy.

"Anything to drink?" Buddy heard her ask six times, routinely and in monotone, before she got to him.

"Well, hello, ma'am, and how are you today?" Buddy replied to the same question.

"I'm fine. Do you want anything to drink?"

"Oh, a fifth cup of coffee would be great, thank you. Black, please. Don't want anything to pollute my coffee," Buddy added with his continued smile.

Jon ordered a coffee as well and Cecelia was about to move on when Buddy asked her again, "Ma'am, are you sure you're okay? You seem a little bothered."

Cecilia glared at Buddy. "Sir, other than having a couple of team members who aren't pulling their weight, and passengers who are preventing me from doing my job, I'm fine, as I clearly told you!"

"Well," Buddy continued kindly, "If I can do anything to help, you know where to find me."

"I don't need any help, thank you," Cecelia said bluntly as she turned to the passengers across the aisle.

Buddy and Jon sat in silence for a few minutes as Cecelia moved to the rows behind them.

"Wow," Jon finally said. "That's not a happy person."

"She doesn't appear so, does she? Must be having a bad day."

"Or a bad life," Jon interjected.

"I don't want to take it that far. Remember, we can't judge because we don't know the whole story. One thing I know is that I don't know everything she's dealing with. What I also know is that she's making whatever is going on in her life worse."

"How so?" Jon asked.

"From our brief encounter, I'd say she blames others for all of her problems, fails to take responsibility for herself, doesn't manage her emotions very well, and believes she doesn't need any help from others."

"Wow. That's quite an observation."

"Well, I could be wrong, but what I am right about is that all of those things I just listed are signs of low self-awareness. She seems to be in a low boil that shows on her face as much as my nose shows on mine. She looks like she could start a fight in an empty house."

Jon laughed. "Buddy, you're a friendly guy, but did you expect her to stop in the middle of doing her job and share her problems with you just because you asked if you could help? I think that's a little unrealistic, don't you?"

"Absolutely!" Buddy agreed. "But there is, 'I don't need any help at this moment because you're a stranger and I'm busy, thank you,' and then there is, 'I don't need help, period.' She seems to be the latter."

Jon reflected on that.

Buddy continued. "And, again, I could be completely wrong about her, but what I believe I am right about is that people who are low in self-awareness are completely wrapped up in their own world, sort of bullying their way through life, and they are convinced they don't need any help. On the other hand, people who are growing in self-awareness, know that they do. We all need it. Like you! And me! Let's get back to that," Buddy said. "And where were we? My mind gets jumping around like grease on a griddle."

"We were discussing that I need to learn everything about me, my personality, strengths, and so forth, then decide what values are important to me and put those in my backpack because they will shape my backpack."

"Good, good," Buddy said.

"And now you were going to tell me what accepting my backpack means."

"Yes, sir. Open the chute!" Buddy declared enthusiastically.

"What?" Jon asked quizzically.

"Maybe, 'Let's rock and roll' would be a better euphemism for you," Buddy said.

"I'm with you now."

"Okay," Buddy continued, "There are many things about ourselves we can change, agreed?"

"Agreed."

"But there are also several things we cannot change."

"Like your height," Jon interjected.

"Well, you can do that, too, with a very expensive and even more painful surgery."

"What?" Jon said amazed.

"Oh, that's a story for when we're sitting around a campfire. Short version is that in a football game my oldest son cracked his growth plate in one leg which stopped that leg from growing. As a result, a few years later his legs were two different lengths. Had surgery to fix it. Craziest thing I ever saw."

"Wow. How is he now?" Jon asked sincerely.

"Oh, he's gooder 'n gold. Decided never to play football again; took up lacrosse instead. A much safer sport," Buddy laughed. "You only get body checked and whacked with sticks in those games!"

"I'm glad he's okay."

"Me and his momma, too!" Buddy exclaimed. "But you're on the right track. There are many things that don't change. You can't change personalities. The psych folks have tried.

"Now mind ya," Buddy looked squarely at Jon. "We shouldn't use our personalities as an excuse for bad behavior. I've seen that more times than Presbyterians take roll. Folks say, 'Oh, I'm just a hothead; that's my personality.' I speak from experience on that one. More on that later."

"Buddy," Jon interrupted, "with your mind bouncing like grease on a whatever you said, I hope you're going to come back to all of those things you said we're going to come back to."

"Me, too." Buddy laughed. "Me, too. And . . . where was I?"

"You were . . ."

"Just kidding, Jon. My memory can feel like I'm climbing a greased pole but I'm good for something that happened 30 seconds ago. Usually." Buddy continued to grin. "I was at things that don't change, like our personality. It is what it is. Even so, we are responsible for our behavior, always.

"In addition, we must accept our past. We can learn from our past and we can make amends for our past, but we can never change it."

"I understand that one," Jon interjected, reflecting on the email fiasco. "And I may need your advice on how to make amends for a mistake I made just this morning."

"I figure we're going to get to all of that, too, Jon. That's going to be the game of life we're all going to play together. For now, I'm setting up the rules. Fair 'nuff?"

"Fair 'nuff," Jon imitated.

"Jon, think of all of the things that we can't change about ourselves: the family we're born into—or lack of family as the case may be—where we were born; those things we are naturally gifted at doing; certain things we like and don't like;

all of our past experiences, good and bad; and of course our physical characteristics, short of surgery, of course." Buddy winked. "What I am coming to realize is those things we cannot change actually are our backpack," Buddy said enthusiastically.

"Okay, you lost me."

"I've lost myself a couple of times today, so you're in good company," Buddy said with a laugh. "Bear with me. Remember, I just started thinking about this backpack idea today. And you're helping me clarify things even more, Jon! Much appreciated!"

"Happy to help," Jon returned the laugh.

"What we have to accept, my friend, is all of those things about us that we cannot change. It's like the old serenity prayer that has been popularized by 12-step groups: God, grant me the serenity to accept the things I cannot change, the courage to change the things I can, and," Buddy paused and looked at Jon.

"And the wisdom to know the difference," Jon concluded.

"Yes, sir. Fact of life. Our personalities, our parents, our past, our certain peculiarities are all things we must accept. They help make us who we are. They are the backpack itself. We get a lot of say about what we put in it and what we want to change about its contents and what we want to take out of it. But our backpack is our backpack."

"*Hmmm.*" Jon reflected.

"Think about this, Jon. One of the many lessons I've learned from a good buddy of mine named Truman is that the surest way to unhappiness is to wish you had someone else's life, someone else's parents or spouse or kids or success or money or past or whatever. We have to accept our stuff. Just like we have to take our own bag from the overhead bin when we leave the plane. We can't take someone else's. Ours is ours.

"To paraphrase: the surest way to unhappiness is to want someone else's backpack. We must accept and learn to celebrate our own backpack!"

Chapter 23

"That's probably another thing I need to be reminded of," Jon said.

"What's that?"

"To not want somebody else's backpack. I constantly compare myself to others; whether it's the money they make, the house they live in, or the car they drive. I even compare my kids' accomplishments to theirs."

"The wide world of competitive parenting," Buddy stated.

"What? Yeah, I haven't heard it described that way, but that gets at it."

"That goes back to our core values," Buddy said. "Nearly every parent on the planet would have 'love my children well' as a basic principle. Yet they need to be reminded that loving our children well means not only instilling our values, educating them, and protecting them, but it also means nurturing them along their pathway, not ours. It means speaking into existence what you see in their life, from their gifts and passions. And it certainly does not mean comparing them with other people's children. Unfortunately, that is rampant. And extremely dangerous for our children.

"Self-awareness includes identifying and living out our own family values, not the proverbial Joneses'. People usually have principles," Buddy continued, "but life, as I said, gets busy, we live life in hurry mode, and we need to be reminded."

"I can certainly understand 'hurry mode,'" Jon said.

"I know," Buddy laughed. "It would seem that *hurry* is one of your core values today!"

Jon smiled, too. "To be honest, hurry seems like it's a core value of mine every day."

"So, you need to be intentional about taking that out of your backpack."

Jon looked at Buddy with a doubtful expression. "Buddy, in today's world, that's like asking me to jump out of this plane and fly."

"Well, son. The world may be in a hurry, but if hurry is getting in the way of me living out my true values, then I've got some decisions to make. That's why this first part of understanding our backpack, after acceptance, includes a decision. What do I want in my backpack, and what do I want to take out or, better, need to take out, to get to the life I really want to lead?"

Jon hung on every word.

"Plus, there's a huge difference between a fast-paced world and a world in a hurry. No doubt the world is going fast and getting faster. Agreed?"

"Agreed," Jon replied.

"But what does *hurry* imply?"

Jon thought. "I guess *hurry* describes someone who is always trying to keep up with the fast-paced world. Or worse, catch up."

"Not a lot of fun, is it?" Buddy stated more than asked.

"No, not at all. Tell me your core values, Buddy."

Buddy thought for a moment. "There are important ones around my marriage and my children that we can discuss later, but I'll share one now that ties into avoiding life in the gear of hurry. You may have heard me and Miss Sofia laugh about the first part of it as we got on the plane."

"I wasn't paying attention to anybody else while I was getting on the plane."

"If that ain't a fact, God's a possum," Buddy belly-laughed. "You were moving like a stumped-tail bull in fly season. Busier than a buzz saw in a lumber yard."

Jon simply stared in amazement.

"So here it is," Buddy continued. "One of my core values is: Enjoy the ride and help as many fellow travelers as I can along the way."

Jon thought about that. "I like that, Buddy. And I would say that you're doing a pretty good job of living that one out."

"Much appreciated. Just know that enjoying the ride doesn't mean I don't get bucked off every once in a while. I've been thrown from more horses than I can remember, literally and figuratively. Life can be tough; you gotta keep getting up and getting back on."

"Agreed," Jon said.

"And to quote another cowboy, John Wayne, 'Life is tough, but it's a lot tougher when you're stupid.'"

Now they both laughed.

"So self-aware people can make mistakes," Jon said. "They only try not to make stupid mistakes?"

"Yup. Especially avoiding the ones that can truly blow up their whole world, at work or home."

"Kind of like I did with my email today. Life is a whole lot tougher now than it would have been. And that stupid mistake was actually due to being in, as you described it, 'hurry mode.'"

Buddy knew they would get to the details of that email soon enough. At the moment, he wanted Jon to understand the power of choice and personal responsibility.

"I don't mind making mistakes," Buddy continued. "I just don't want to keep making the same mistakes. Or mistakes that, had I slowed down enough and thought through the consequences, I would have never made in the first place. Regardless, I am always responsible for my mistakes."

"Again, touché," Jon smiled. "I get it. Self-aware people own their mistakes."

"And much, much more," Buddy added.

"For example?" Jon asked.

"Can I make an observation about something you said awhile back?"

Jon couldn't think of anything too dangerous in what he had said.

"Sure."

"You stated that your wife 'made you mad,' right?"

Jon breathed a sigh of relief. He thought he was safe here. He was, of course, wrong.

"Yeah, she did. But believe me—" Jon thought he needed to defend the way he treated his wife, "that was minor. Grace and I have a great marriage. She was the least of all the things that have made me mad today. Alarm clocks, kids out of bed, idiot drivers, bozos who don't know which side of the moving walkway to stand on, and certainly my boss." Jon was somewhat proud of himself for having a quick defense for his anger.

"I even busted up my foot by tripping over my own backpack," Jon offered before he realized his own reference and thought he may have set himself up to get another "*Hmmm.*"

Buddy chose to ignore the backpack reference—for the moment. "Well," Buddy started, "no one or no thing, for that matter, can really 'make you mad.'" Jon started to interrupt and defend himself further when Buddy held up his hand. "Please, before you respond, let me ask you a hypothetical.

"Let's say you are rushing through the airport, which," Buddy grinned and winked at Jon, "really isn't a hypothetical." Jon had to smile, too. "So, you're hurrying along and another person in that same hurry-gear comes around a corner and crashes into you. As a result, your backpack flies off of your shoulder, hits the ground, and all of the contents spill out all over the terminal. You got that picture?"

"Yes, and, again, that's not a hypothetical," Jon warily replied.

Buddy smiled at that, too.

"So, here's the $9.99 question." Buddy paused and looked straight at Jon and asked, "Where did all of that stuff, which is now all over the floor, come from?"

Jon replied, "Inside my backpack."

Chapter 24

"What are you two talking about now?" Sofia asked as she returned to Buddy and Jon's row. As crew lead, she enjoyed taking the time on long flights to walk the aisle and simply connect with passengers, especially her friends.

Buddy smiled up at Sofia. "Jon was starting to explain to me how his wife 'made him mad' this morning."

Sofia knew where this conversation was going. She had heard Buddy say on more than one occasion that "'You make me so angry' is the most misused phrase on the planet." It was a truth she had shared with many others herself.

Jon ignored Sofia for the moment because he was still processing Buddy's spilled-backpack scenario. "Okay, Buddy, so what you are saying with your not-so-hypothetical hypothetical is that if I become angry and that anger pours out, it is because the anger was already inside me. Well of course that makes sense. I am the one defending myself with my anger, so it comes from me."

Buddy briefly recapped the backpack illustration to get Sofia up to speed in the conversation. Then he turned back to Jon, who was looking rather impatient.

"*Hmm*. No, that's not quite it," Buddy replied. "I am saying that all of the stuff spilled out hither, thither, and yon on the floor is only dressed up to look like anger. It is actually a whole mess of broken beliefs and mislabeled emotions.

113

Anger is the emotion that the person who owns the backpack chooses to display, consciously or not, because of that mess. That anger is almost always a secondary emotion that gets vomited up because the angry individual has not dealt with their own mess."

Jon's face continued to show every emotion he was feeling, and the predominant look at this point was confusion. Sofia knew that Buddy could get so excited that his southern drawl hit 90 miles per hour and listeners were struggling to keep up.

"Jon, if I may," Sofia began. "First of all, Buddy, I love the backpack idea! Every single flight I am on there is somebody, and it's usually a lot of somebodys, who are hitting other passengers with their backpacks."

"The correct term is *whacking*," Buddy interjected with a smile. "And thank you."

"Jon, how would you define anger?" Sofia continued.

"Well? *Hmm*." With the way the conversation was going, Jon was pretty sure he was going to be wrong no matter what he said. That was a new feeling for him. A lack of confidence in his answers. "I would say that anger is a strong emotion resulting from something happening that you don't like," Jon stated, trying to sound confident.

Sofia and Buddy continued to look at Jon intently, but neither said anything.

"It's a lot of things. Like that emotion you have when things don't go like they should, or when people don't do what they're supposed to do." Jon paused. They listened. "Or what happens when you hit your finger with a hammer."

"Or trip over your own backpack," Buddy interjected with a smile.

"Yes," Jon smiled back. "Or that."

"You're kind of throwing horseshoes blindfolded hoping to hit a ringer, aren't you?" Buddy grinned.

"Maybe," Jon smiled back. "But those are all things that make me angry, that's for sure."

Buddy looked up at Sofia, wanting her to continue.

"All of those are certainly part of what people do when they feel angry. As you said, those are some things that make you angry. But those are responses, not a definition of anger," Sofia pointed out.

"Then enlighten me," Jon said.

"Okay, I'll try," Sofia began. "First of all, yes, anger is an emotion. And it is one of the core emotions experienced by all human beings. As such, anger in and of itself is not wrong."

"I know," Jon interrupted. "I've always felt that my angry responses were justified."

"*Hmm*," Jon heard from Buddy, almost under his breath.

Sofia continued. "I said that as an *emotion*, there was nothing inherently wrong with anger. What we *do* with that emotion, however, is another story. Let's nail down a definition. Most medical doctors are going to define it based on what your body physically does when the emotion of anger is present. That's true, but incomplete. Mental health professionals usually add that its origin is in feeling that someone or something has in some way deliberately wronged you."

"I was pretty close," Jon said, looking over at Buddy. And looking back at Sofia, he added, "And I suppose that, like Buddy, you know all of this because you read a lot of books?"

"And listen to podcasts, watch Ted Talks, whatever I can find. I also love learning from my passengers. As you can imagine, I've met doctors and psychologists and I've asked them." Sofia paused. "Plus, I was having this conversation with my crew mates earlier today."

"Wow! Okay. I feel like there was a 'but' coming after that last statement," Jon said.

"It's more of an 'and,'" Sofia continued. "That strong physiological reaction and the perception of being wronged grow from the feeling that you have experienced an injustice of some kind. But the real question becomes: What is truly an injustice? And does the intensity of the anger match the depth of the perceived injustice?"

It was Jon's turn to listen.

"Jon, someone threatening your family and your responding in fight mode brought on by anger is a just cause. Becoming angry when you hear of child abuse, sexual slavery, hungry children, abused women, terrorist attacks, genocide, and many other social issues is not only understandable, it is normal for someone who is emotionally mature and intelligent. We want the cruel inequity made right. Do you agree with that?"

"Of course," Jon responded, rather indignantly. "You'd have to be a complete bonehead not to!"

"Agreed. But what about other events or even people that, again as you would say, 'make you' angry? Is a traffic jam a justice issue? Is losing your keys, a barista making a mistake on your latte, lines at airports, or being late for a plane a life-threatening situation? An issue of justice that deserves an extremely angry response?"

Jon sat silently.

"Miss Sofia, you certainly live up to your name: 'Sofia, the wise one,'" Buddy said.

Sofia blushed.

"And thanks for making sense of my twang! My wife tells me that my brain can get moving faster than small-town gossip at the barbershop, and my lips are still trying to catch up to yesterday."

"Buddy," Jon said, "I never quite know what's going to come out of your mouth."

"My wife says that, too," Buddy smiled.

"Bottom line is this," Buddy summarized, "broken beliefs are simply wrong beliefs. They're misaligned priorities that grow out of own selfishness. Beliefs that you shouldn't be inconvenienced or ever have to wait or be negatively impacted by others' mistakes are simply wrong-headed."

"For some, anger simply shows up when people disagree with them," Sofia continued. "When they get pushed on, they push back even harder. Again, the response is disproportionate to the stimulus."

"Jon," Buddy continued, "we have the power of choice. We can change those beliefs. But we have to first own the fact that those broken beliefs don't lie in another person or the situation. They are tucked firmly away in our own backpack."

Chapter 25

"So," Jon began, "What you're telling me is that if Grace does anything that results in my being angry, that it's my fault and not hers. Is that right?"

"Close," Buddy replied.

"But if anger is only an emotion and, as you said, Sofia, neither right nor wrong, then how is the emotion my fault?"

"Great question!" Buddy responded. "And that's why I said you were close."

Sofia knew she had other responsibilities, so simply said, "Boys, I need to move on and will join back in later. And Jon, that is a great question. I will answer with a comment and a question. The emotion may not always be a choice, but what you do next, is."

Jon thought about that. "And the question?"

"Were you consciously aware of the emotion to begin with?" Sofia paused. "Bye for now."

"Adios, kiddo," Buddy said as Sofia walked away. "Boy, I sure do like that gal. She is one great individual. And her husband, Scott, ain't too bad, either, though I think that most of his positive qualities come from being married to her. And believe me," Buddy stated emphatically, "I am preaching to the mirror on that one."

Jon half smiled at the comment but wanted to get back to Sofia's words. Almost the entirety of his morning had been lived in a state of anger—from getting up late to the dog toy to the email to parking places to . . . to his backpack—and he had justified that anger because of the things, and the people, that had happened to him. They may not rise to the level of a major world injustice, but aren't these events that make everyone angry?

More than justifying the anger, he had justified all of his actions.

And was he aware he was angry? What kind of question was that?

"Buddy, I'll admit that I may overreact on occasion, but wouldn't anybody who had a morning like mine get mad? And I haven't even told you about the email storm that my boss caused that will probably result in my losing a promotion or even my job. And it's not like I went road rage on anybody, so I think I'm in fairly good control of things."

"*Hmm,*" Buddy started. "Where to begin with all of that?"

Jon knew it was time to be quiet. And listen.

"Jon, I've got a good friend named Josiah; now Josiah is so honest you could shoot craps with him over the phone."

Jon smiled again.

"He'll tell you the honest-truth, good or bad, yet do it with kindness. But just as important, he is honest with himself. He's got a hat and cattle. No pretentiousness. When he screws up, he admits it. Immediately. Without excuse."

Jon wondered about that. That didn't describe him.

"For example, last week he was supposed to meet me for coffee to talk over a land deal. Bottom line is that he didn't show because he plumb forgot. Called me about 15 minutes after he was supposed to be there to offer one sincere apology."

Buddy stared ahead and continued. "He could have blamed a hundred things for forgetting or, like most, tried to justify his mistake by going on and on about all he had going on. And believe me, running 450 head of cattle and often wrangling 12 grandchildren, he's got plenty going on. Didn't blame any of that. Took responsibility and apologized. Didn't even tell me why he forgot, which, if I was to guess—which is dangerous, I know—it's because he's trying to use the calendar on that new fangled phone his kids got him instead of the one hanging by his backdoor that he gets every year for free from the feed store."

"That really doesn't describe me," Jon thought.

"Now with me it was no big deal; we've been through more life together than a band of brothers. And sitting and having a cup of coffee at Louella's Cafe is never a waste of time. But Josiah would have acted the same way if he forgot an appointment with the Governor of Texas."

Jon knew where this was heading but asked anyway. "What's your point, Buddy?"

"Did your boss's email truly cause all of these problems you're referring to?"

"Well," Jon began, his voice rising, "it certainly all started with an email he sent before 6:00 a.m. that set the tone for everything that happened afterwards."

"So, is that the email where he said your promotion and your job are in jeopardy?" Buddy queried.

Jon started to speak, then thought better of it. He knew he had exaggerated.

"Jon," Buddy continued, "I'm not really interested in what you did or didn't do. And I really don't care a gnat's eyelash what your boss did. What I do care about is you. And I can't care about you and not tell you the truth, especially when I believe it will help you. There may be some truth that needs to be left unsaid, but this ain't it. You need a truth-teller!"

Buddy looked Jon straight in the eye.

"Your boss may have sent the first email; he may have sent it at an inopportune time. He could have said you're on thin ice or even fired. Heck, he might'a said, 'Jon, you're the biggest bozo on the planet with an IQ only rivaled by the bucket on a backhoe.' And, as Miss Sofia said, all of those are events that could contribute to your emotion of anger; your perception of being unjustly treated."

Jon listened. He knew there would be an *and*.

"And yet none of those things caused your reaction. Jon, here's another fact of life: You can't control what others do to you. But you do control whatever you do next because whatever you do next is your choice. So, every response you made after your boss typed whatever he typed is—"

"My responsibility," Jon finished, somewhat embarrassed.

"Sometimes we make good choices; sometimes not," Buddy continued. "Either way, every human being on the planet is responsible for their choices, for what comes out of their backpack."

"So, this is number two, I take it," said Jon, working to make the bright light on him a little dimmer. "One is to know which backpack is ours, decide what we want in it, and accept it. Then, two is taking responsibility for it at all times, right?"

"Right as rain, Lucky," Buddy replied.

"So, what about the question that Sofia asked? About whether I was aware of the emotions I was feeling? How does that tie in?"

"Jon, if I had called you at, say, 6:30 this morning, and asked, 'Jon, are you angry?' What would you have said?"

"Dang right I'm angry," Jon quickly replied.

"Then what if I asked, 'So, Jon . . . what are you going to do with that awareness?'"

Once more, Jon started to say something and stopped. He realized he was again going to justify his actions because he was angry.

"Jon, self-aware people always try to answer this very important question: 'What am I feeling right now?' Then they answer the vital follow-up question: 'What am I going to do with that emotion?'"

Jon thought about that.

"To put it another way," Buddy continued, "since I'm responsible for everything in my backpack, wouldn't it be wise to work to be aware of what's going on inside it? And then, since it impacts everyone around me, shouldn't I work hard to manage what comes out of my backpack?"

Chapter 26

Cecelia was making her way back down the aisle, this time delivering drinks.

"Thank you, ma'am," Buddy kindly stated as she returned to their row.

Cecelia set the coffee down gruffly and said nothing.

As she was once more out of earshot, Jon stated, "Again, wow. That is one angry individual."

"*Hmmm.*" Buddy started. Jon waited.

"She appears that way," Buddy agreed, surprising Jon. "However, I'd bet dollars to dumplings that if you asked her if she was angry, she'd say, 'no.'"

"What makes you say that?"

"Well, our friend there, bless her heart, seems pretty low in self-awareness as I said earlier. Unaware of her backpack, you might say. Along with all of the other stuff we've talked about, other signs of low self-awareness include holding a grudge—she apparently was still annoyed with me for what she interpreted as prying—and denying your anger altogether. I'd wager that if you asked her, she would say she is not angry because she does not get angry because she interprets anger as bad."

Jon thought about that, and the times he would declare to others, including Grace, that he most certainly was not angry . . . as his voice raised and his teeth clenched.

"A few minutes ago," Buddy continued, "I asked if you would say you were angry if I called you early this morning. You enthusiastically said . . ." Buddy looked at Jon and paused.

"Dang right!" Jon said proudly, but with a smile.

"As we discussed, handling your anger wrong and blaming others for it is a problem. But so is completely denying your anger."

Buddy paused to let that sink in.

"Jon, self-aware people—those who know their backpack, what's in it, and where it is—are not only good at managing their emotions, they are also, even before that, good at labeling their emotions. Which is also a learned process."

"Go on," Jon asked.

Buddy thought for a moment. "Okay," he continued, "in Texas, as you know, we love to barbecue. I don't mean only eat it; I mean cook it. It's actually a requirement for State citizenship," Buddy said with a serious enough look Jon decided not to question him.

"Jon, when you are first learning your way around a grill, it's difficult to barbecue if your spices aren't labeled. After some practice, which includes overcooking a few pieces of brisket, you know your cumin from your cayenne pepper without a thought. Which, if you can't or don't tell them apart, you'll have some surprised, if not hurting, guests.

"Labeling things correctly is critical."

Jon started to ask what the heck he was talking about now, but then it hit him. As with all his cowboy euphemisms, Buddy made sense. At least, if you thought about it long enough.

Jon gave a knowing nod to Buddy.

"Can we get on to that third part? About knowing exactly how our backpack impacts some people around us?" Jon asked. "Observing our flight attendant there is bringing that into focus for me. Along with thinking about how people may be affected by me mixing up my spices," Jon smiled.

"Absolutely," Buddy said. "Except it is not some people; it's everybody."

"What?" Jon queried.

"Our backpack impacts everybody. You said, 'Some people.' In reality, our backpacks impact every single person in our path."

"But," Jon pushed back, "You said I only hit every other person on that side of the plane," Jon pointed. "How did I impact those I didn't hit?"

"That's the question, isn't it, Jon?"

Jon thought about that.

"You don't have to whack them to impact them. It may be neutral, like the ones you didn't whack," Buddy laughed. "Or it may be positive. Some probably saw you coming and were thrilled that you didn't whack them!"

"Positive impact. Like you with me," Jon said without thinking.

"Well, Lucky, I certainly hope so. I certainly hope so."

Jon started to ask about being called Lucky, but Buddy interrupted his thought with a question.

"As I've been thinking about this today, the illustrations just keep pouring into my big 'ol head. Jon, have you ever been to the Metropolitan Museum of Art in New York City?"

"I have," Jon replied. "My wife loves that place."

"My bride and I do, too. Filled with the works of so many creative, talented artists. I mean, I can't do color-by-numbers without messing up, so I'm in awe of their skill."

Jon nodded in agreement.

"And do you remember what they make you do if you are carrying a backpack when you walk in that grand place?"

Jon thought for a moment. "I do! They make you wear it on your front. Grace had a pack slung over one shoulder when we arrived and that's how the staff asked her to carry it as we wandered through the museum."

"That's right!" Buddy continued, "And do you know why?"

"*Uh-huh.* I thought it was silly at first, so I asked. It's so visitors don't accidentally hit a priceless piece of art with it."

"Right again!" Buddy said. "And how smart is that! I did a little research today as I was waiting at the gate."

"I wish I had had time to wait at the gate today," Jon interrupted.

Buddy smiled, "Hang on, Lucky. We'll get to that, too."

"What I found," Buddy continued, "is that there are over two million works of art in the Met's collection, and, as you said, many of them priceless. When people are carrying their packs on their backs, they are usually only semiconscious of having them on. They could quickly turn while in a conversation, or when they get excited about a piece of art, or simply when walking down the aisles between statutes. They don't hit objects intentionally, they are simply unaware of what their backpack is doing."

"Kind of like that lady," Jon paused, "And me, I guess— when we were walking down the aisle of the plane."

"Exactamundo, Jon. Being forced to wear your backpack on the front forces you to be aware of it at all times. Self-awareness means I am aware of myself at all times, that I am responsible for myself at all times, and I know how I am impacting others . . ."

"At all times," Jon finished the sentence.

"Fact of life," Buddy said. "With no or even limited self-awareness, you are constantly and unknowingly impacting others, sometimes positively and often negatively, with your backpack."

Chapter 27

"Okay," Jon began, "I am starting to understand that my backpack and all that is in it and all that it does is my responsibility."

"Good for you!" Buddy exclaimed, once again with a big smile on his face.

"But this all seems pretty daunting," Jon stated. "I have to label emotions, evaluate how they impact me, fix my broken beliefs, get angry for the right reasons, and not hurt people. And I'm sure I left something out. All while simply trying to get through my day and get my work done. Or even dealing with my kids around home. If all of that were even possible, which I'm not sure about, it still sounds very complicated."

Buddy reflected a moment. "Riding a horse can sound complicated at first, not to mention frightening that you're going to climb on a 1000-pound-plus animal known for ditching cowboys. But once you get the basics down, it is not that hard. From there, you're simply perfecting your craft."

"I think professional cowboys and cowgirls might disagree with you if you're trying to make what they do sound easy," Jon said, trying to sound like he knew a little bit about being a cowboy, even if he knew nothing about cows.

"Oh, they wouldn't say it was easy. But they wouldn't say it was complicated, either," Buddy said confidently. "They would say what they do is difficult and takes skill, years of practice, and a lot of time spent on their head in the dirt. Which, by the way, is also what a good psychologist or a seasoned, people-skilled leader might say. But the basics are not complicated. They may be difficult to master; they take lots of practice, but riding a horse is not complicated."

Buddy let that sink in before he continued. "For the cowboy, it starts with asking the right questions. Am I on the right horse for my ability? Are the stirrups set at the right length? Do I understand the basic commands and reign movements and are they in conjunction with one another? Am I connecting with my horse and is my horse connecting with me? It's asking the right questions, getting coaching and input from others, and practicing till it becomes almost automatic. Then you practice some more.

"Self-awareness takes practice, Jon. Lots and lots of practice. Continuous practice. Never-ending practice. And still, we will never be perfect and there will always be those occasions where our words or actions hurt others. We'll end up off the horse on our heads in the dirt.

"But wouldn't it be great," Buddy continued, again looking Jon directly in the eye, "if we could hurt people less? And hurt less people? And, simultaneously, help and care for more people?"

A brief smile came across Jon's face as he thought about that. "It certainly would," he said as he reflected on his morning. "It most certainly would."

Buddy felt a hand on his shoulder and turned to be greeted by Sofia's warm smile. "Can I get you two gentlemen anything else?"

"I could use a re-do of the whole day," Jon said, half-joking and more-than-half serious.

"Then take one," Sofia smiled.

"*Huh?*" Jon said, looking at Buddy, then back at Sofia. "I thought Buddy said that one of those things we have to accept about our backpacks is our past. Because we can't do anything to change it. So how can I get a re-do?"

Sofia smiled and rested her arm on the top of Buddy's seat. "When my kids were younger, they would, on occasion, barge through the door after school with a—well, let's just call it, a poor attitude."

"A horn-tossing mood," Buddy interjected. "That's another cattle reference," Buddy winked at Jon.

"That would describe it," Sofia continued. "And before they got to their second or third complaint, I would simply say, 'Re-do.'"

"So, they had to change the way they complained? And not blame others like we discussed?" Jon asked.

"There was a little more to it than that," Sofia continued. "They would have to turn around, leave the house, walk back to the corner where the bus dropped them off, then walk back home."

"Wow. Hardcore," Jon observed.

"Not really, Jon. Maybe ten minutes total. But it wasn't about the walk. It was about them taking time to consciously reflect on their current emotional state, their mood, and reminding themselves that they can control their response and their words, regardless of their mood."

"The question you asked me earlier," Jon interrupted, "about being aware of my emotions."

"Exactly," Sofia continued. "Our kids learned that they could come home with a more positive attitude and not vomit their negativity all over everyone at home, if you'll pardon the graphic analogy," Sofia laughed.

"Aren't you then asking them to be fake?" Jon queried. "And not share about the bad parts of their day? Don't parents want to hear about the good and bad from their kids?"

Buddy was watching this conversation like a ping-pong match, smiling and loving every minute of it. "This is more fun than watching a rodeo clown on fire, isn't it?" Buddy stated, with that kid-with-cotton-candy smile on his face.

"What do you mean by fun?'" Jon replied. "Like a root canal is fun?" Jon tried to joke. "I like the idea of hurting less people, but this conversation has also brought up regrets about how I behaved this morning, and most of my life, for that matter." Jon stared out the window of the plane. "This hasn't been a whole lot of fun yet."

"Emphasis on the *yet*, Jon. We'll get to it. But I rudely interrupted Miss Sofia. Thoughts pop into my head and I have trouble not saying them. My bride chides me for that all the time. Low self-control. And there I go again . . . Miss Sofia?"

"Thank you, old friend, and I certainly don't consider you rude. So back to you, Jon. Wonderful question," Sofia continued. "It may seem like you're asking them to deny their feelings and pretend to be happy even if they're not, at least at first. But in the end, it's completely the opposite. Self-aware, or should I say, *backpack-aware* people are first and foremost honest about their current emotional state. They can answer the question . . ."

"What am I feeling right now?" Jon interrupted.

"Exactly, Jon. You have been learning!" Sofia exclaimed as she winked at Buddy. Buddy grinned. "And then the next question after that?"

"What am I going to do about it?" Jon answered.

Then he paused and reflected. "But isn't, 'What do I want to do about it?' actually a better question? Because I can imagine that there are times that my answer to that first question would be, 'Nothing,' simply because I want to be in a bad mood."

Buddy's head turned back toward Sofia.

"And that, my young friend, is exactly the point of my kids' re-do. On the first walk home, they let the circumstances of their day dictate their behavior. That horrible teacher X, that backstabbing friend Y, or that mean bus driver Z. As such, their emotions influenced their attitude, which had already decided what their behavior was going to be without them even thinking about it.

"On the re-do walk, they had a chance to decide: Is what's happening in my backpack going to be the final determiner of what comes out of my backpack? As a parent, I most definitely wanted to hear about the teacher and the friend and the bus driver. But I wanted them to know that they had the ability to understand how their emotions were impacting them and then choose their behavior accordingly."

"So, what if they wanted to stay in their bad mood, and only complain?" Jon asked, not so dispassionately.

"Oh, then they made the choice of me not hearing them complain, because that would be my choice," Sofia replied. "I would simply say, come back when you can talk about it but not gripe and grumble about it. And honestly, I rarely had to make that last statement."

They all stayed quiet for a while. Letting it all soak in.

Buddy broke the silence.

"Jon, a few minutes ago you said that you were beginning to understand that you are responsible for everything in your backpack and everything that comes out of your backpack."

"Yes, I did."

"The next big step, the step that takes all of the practice we were discussing, is realizing that our emotions need not be the excuse for our bad behavior. We can, for the most part, decide what actually does come out of our backpack."

Chapter 28

The plane droned on.

Sofia edged around so a few passengers who were headed to the lavatory could get past.

From Sofia's angle, Cecelia seemed to be hiding in the galley, scrolling through her phone.

Collin was busy talking and laughing with passengers, practicing skills he had received in coaching from Sofia.

Buddy waited.

This time Jon broke the silence.

"Can we get back to that fun part? Don't get me wrong, Buddy and Sofia," he added looking up at her. "I have thoroughly enjoyed getting to know you both, and, I must admit, simply talking about all of this seems to have lowered my stress and anxiety level, though I'm not sure why."

"We can get to that, too," Sofia threw in. "There is a *why*."

"Yes, siree," Buddy joined in. "With our stress, emotions, responses, and the whole kit and kaboodle we've been discussing, there is always a *why*. Sometimes that *why* might be that we overstuffed ourselves at Bubba's Barbecue Buffet, but there is always a reason. But I tell ya, Jon. I'm as happy as a puppy in a preschool that you're aware of your change in stress level. That means you're paying attention to what's going on inside your backpack. Which, by the way, is the only way to manage what comes out of your backpack."

It was Jon's turn to say, "*Hmmm.*" But it wasn't because he was going to tell Buddy he was wrong. Rather, it was affirmation that he was continuing to see how Buddy was right.

"Jon, I know you have children because you referred to dealing with them around home," Buddy paused, "Not to mention that you shared about wiping one out with your backpack this morning. A suitable metaphor if I've ever heard one," Buddy said with his uninterrupted grin.

Jon had to laugh at that, too.

"Yes, I have three. Annalise is ten, Jaxx is eight, and little Lilly is four."

"A blessed man," Buddy observed. "I'm guessing you're pretty durn grateful for them, huh?"

Jon paused and then reflected out loud. "Yes. Yes, I am, Buddy. I am blessed and I am grateful."

"I have no doubt." Buddy continued, "Jon, do you remember when Annalise, Jaxx, and little Lilly were first learning that they could do things? Discovering that they had some power over their environment? They could throw their food on the ground; they could bang their cup against the tray to make a loud noise. They could reach for you and you would pick them up."

Jon reflected, gratefully, on his family. "Sure," he replied. "Those were always fun times."

"Nailed it!" Buddy exclaimed.

"*Huh?*" Jon started to question, but then an understanding look came across his face. "This 'fun as a rodeo clown' thing for you, Buddy, is that you enjoy learning, and seeing people learn? Is that right? And maybe that you even see me as a little child, learning all of these new things?" Jon wasn't sure how Buddy would answer.

"No, Jon, I certainly don't see you as a child. But, you're right, it was fun learning when we were children. And, if we embrace it, it is fun learning now. It is fun when we know that we have a choice over the environment of ourselves. We have choices about our backpack. You, my friend, are continuing to discover the power of choice. And that is even more fun because you can know that, as you practice, you will hurt Grace, your precious children, your friends, and even those you work with—those who got that email this morning—*less*," Buddy said as he nudged Jon. "You will hurt them all less. And you will make them feel loved even more."

"Jon," Sofia joined in, "understanding the power of choice is so incredibly empowering. Remember when we were discussing anger earlier? We said we can always choose how we respond to others."

"I get that," Jon replied, "now." He was agitated again. He was struggling to wrap his head around all that he was responsible for—and still wrestling with what he wasn't.

"Buddy, a few minutes ago you said that everybody should live as if they are wearing their backpacks on their front, as required at the Met Museum, so people don't accidentally whack priceless art objects."

"*Ooo*, I love that place," Sofia chimed in, "And I like where this is going!"

Buddy nodded, looked up at Sofia, and gave a friendly wink.

"But I think you'll admit that outside of the Met, that's simply impractical. I mean, what is the first thing people do after they leave the museum? They immediately move their backpack back around to the back because, after all, it's not a *front*pack, it is a *back*pack!" Jon stated emphatically, rather proud of himself for his wit and pushback.

He was also feeling that he needed to defend himself, as well as make the case that nobody can be fully aware of or in control of their backpack at all times. "And let's go back to kids having fun learning; one of the ways they learn is that they make a lot of mistakes. When they're learning to walk, they fall down a lot. As a matter of fact, I have a scar above my eye from where I fell into the corner of a table when I was learning to walk. I don't remember it, frankly, but I doubt I thought it was much fun at the time."

Jon knew he was rambling, but he was also trying to move the spotlight off of him and feel a little better about his own role in this crazy day. "So, how can someone, with a backpack on their back where it belongs, not make mistakes? And how on earth can they always know how that backpack is impacting others? And how is all of that fun?" Jon finished, somewhat proudly.

"Once again," Sofia said, "All great questions. First, I'd say this is not about never making mistakes. That's impossible. But it is about making fewer mistakes."

"And learning so we don't make the same mistakes twice . . . or at least too many times," Buddy threw in.

"Right," Sofia continued. "Jon, I noticed when you entered the plane and then made it to your seat, you walked."

She paused a moment.

"No disrespect, Sofia, but that's kind of the epitome of obvious, isn't it?"

"Agreed," Sofia said. "But that may not have seemed obvious to the child who was no doubt bleeding from his head after he fell into a table."

Now Jon listened.

"If I had asked you back then, 'Little Jon, do you want to try and walk again?' and you were able to articulate a response, you most likely would have said . . . "

Jon said nothing for a moment.

"Not being perfect is no excuse for not trying to get better, is it?" Jon finally responded.

"Well said, both of you," Buddy joined in. "There are a few types of folks that really get my quills up, but," Buddy gave Jon a nudge and a wink, "they're still my quills and I'm responsible for who I stick with them."

Jon winked back.

Buddy continued, "One of them is the person who decides to stop learning and growing. It's like they think they know everything they need to know. They deflect or argue with feedback. They justify all of their mistakes. They blame everyone and everything but themselves. They refuse to grasp that when it comes to life and their backpack, they've got to keep learning. If we're going to make this world work, then whether I've whacked you one time or seventy-seven times, as a part of this-here human race, I need to keep trying to whack you less with my backpack."

Chapter 29

Sofia shared her "See you laters" and headed toward the galley. As he watched her go, Jon reflected on his recent observations of Sofia. Whether she was carrying a tray of drinks, a passenger's luggage, or just herself, she never hit anyone with her stuff.

"I wish I had more help in learning not to whack others," Jon said, half under his breath.

"Well, Jon," Buddy continued, "who helped you when you did try and walk again, which you obviously did?"

"My parents, I guess. I'm sure they provided balance. I know I did for my kids."

"Absolutely! Your parents provided direction in many ways, undoubtedly. And who else gave you input in your life?"

"Teachers, coaches, my boss Vera, whom I was telling you about."

"Think of all of the people that—"

"I get it," Jon interrupted, with yet another *aha* moment. "We learn how we are impacting others—and how our backpack is impacting others—with help from others."

"Bull's-eye!" Buddy said. "Jon, one of the absolute most important questions that must be answered if you want to truly be a leader, heck, if you want to be fully human, is simply this: Am I coachable?" He let the question sink in.

"Remember what we said a few minutes ago? No one knows what it's truly like to be you. And at the same time—"

"You don't know what it's like for others to be with you," Jon finished.

"That's a fact of life," Buddy punctuated.

He let that sink in, again, too.

"Jon, we all need feedback; me, you, Sofia, the pilot, everyone on this plane. Because, as you rightly pointed out, our backpacks are on our backs. Combine that with the fact that most folks are living life faster than a prairie fire with a tailwind, distracted by more gadgets than James Bond on Christmas morning, and people are going to get backpack-whacked. We need help. We need 360-degree feedback. Without it, we're only pretending to be self-aware at best."

That was also sinking in.

"Another fact of life," Buddy added. "The only folks who are really stuck are those who don't think they need feedback. What they are really saying is, 'I don't want to change. I'm good where I am.' It's the Popeye syndrome: 'I yam what I yam.' And often, the yammers are the ones that blame every problem in their life on the weather or their raising. They simply don't take responsibility for their own life."

Buddy looked back at Jon. "I'll bet dollars to donuts that your children love learning new things. Am I right?"

"Oh, sure. The oldest sometimes thinks she doesn't need to learn everything that her teachers want her to, but, yes, they all enjoy learning." Jon paused. "I'm guessing that Lilly, the four-year-old, is learning to stay out of the way of my backpack," he added with a smile.

Buddy laughed out loud.

"That's for durn sure, my friend!"

"It doesn't matter if it's a child or a foal," Buddy said, still grinning, "Young-'uns are always eager to learn, to try, and to fail—and to get up and try again. The problem is a whole mess of adults seem to lose that passion for growth as they get older."

"I don't think that's true," Jon pushed back. "Every company I've worked for has had some sort of an annual performance review. I always get told what I'm doing well and where I need to improve."

"Son, it would take a whole 'nuther plane ride to discuss all of the problems with the way most companies do annual performance reviews."

"Well, Buddy, no offense, but from our discussion—and now that I think about it, it's amazing we haven't had the 'What do you do for a living?' conversation, I'm assuming you're a rancher, so I'm not really sure how you know very much about performance reviews, beyond reviewing cowboys at a rodeo."

"Fair question, Jon. And I'm as thick-skinned as a momma alligator. No offense taken. And, you're right. Ranching is most of what I do now. But before that I also ran a pretty good size midstream oil company. Since I got out of that role, I've sat on several boards of companies, both profit and non. I've had my fair share of discussions, and done my fair share of research, on the topic of performance reviews."

"Wow!" Jon replied, with an obviously surprised look. "I had no idea. I mean, I liked you before and respected your opinion, but now I'm impressed."

"Don't be. That and five bucks will get me a cup of coffee at the boutique coffeeshop. A small one, anyway. Jon, to tell you the truth, what turns my crank is companies who care about leadership. That's what companies need: leadership development. And it needs to start at the top. And numero uno in leadership development is self-awareness. Which does not come, if I may add, from typical performance reviews."

Jon was about to push back again when Buddy asked him another question.

"Let me ask you, Jon: How many significant, life-improving changes have you made because of a performance review?"

Jon thought. Hard. And long.

"Well . . . I'm frequently told I'm disorganized or can be too abrasive with some people."

"And was there ever any direction on ways to improve?"

"You mean like take a time-management class or something like that? Sure."

"And did you only hear that type of feedback once a year?"

"Usually."

"And have you made any life-altering improvements in those or any other areas?"

Jon sat in silence.

"The word *annual* is the first part of the problem. I'm guessing that famed UCLA coach, John Wooden, gave feedback to his basketball players more than once a year. A second problem is that the feedback typically comes from one person, your manager. Third, that one person is giving you what *they* think you need. Even if your review is approved by senior leadership, it is still their perspective of what *they think* you need to develop. And they always have to come up with something. They can't give you review without pointing to something you're not doing well. And finally, rarely does their feedback include a clearly defined, actionable behavior that you can change. Now, I'm not saying that's all wrong, but for true life change, the one getting the feedback needs to ask for the feedback they need on a very regular basis."

"I'm lost again. I'm supposed to tell my company how they should be evaluating me?"

"What I'm talking about is much bigger than job performance."

"I'm still lost."

"Jon, I'm just wondering, when was the last time you walked out of a meeting and immediately turned to a colleague and asked, 'Tell me one thing I could have done better in that meeting'? When have you asked someone to help you be a better teammate at the office, or a better husband or a better dad?

"When was the last time you asked yourself, 'I wonder what part of this conflict is mine?' Or thought, 'I'm really angry right now, I need to get some feedback and figure out why?' Have you ever asked someone who knows you well, 'What is one behavior I could stop or start doing that would make your life better?'"

Buddy paused and looked off into space.

"Now that's one eye-opening question." Buddy said. "Actually, it's the answers you receive that are eye-opening."

Buddy looked across the empty seat and straight into Jon's eyes. "Have you ever given anyone permission to be a real truth-teller in your life, Jon? To call you out when you needed it, because of the negative way you were impacting them or others? Because you were whacking someone with your backpack?"

Jon didn't say anything. He did think that Grace had played that role, whether he had actually ever given her permission or not.

"Yes, sir," Buddy continued. "This is so much more than an annual performance review. This is about ongoing feedback on behaviors I need to change. People who are unwilling to get regular, candid feedback and make adjustments from that feedback are unfit for leadership. Leadership starts with self-awareness and self-awareness grows with honest-to-goodness, down-to-brass-tacks feedback about my own backpack."

Chapter 30

They sat in silence for what seemed like hours of grueling interrogation under intense bright lights shining right in Jon's face.

It was more like four minutes and Buddy had been looking around at other people, always with a smile and nod.

Jon finally gave his backpack a little kick.

"So, what do I do now, Buddy? That thing sure has caused me lots of problems this morning. Both metaphorically and in reality."

Buddy listened. There was no question that Jon had Buddy's complete, undivided attention. He reflected on how that made him feel cared for. Buddy was a great listener.

"I've started crafting an email response in my head," Jon continued. "I understand now that my boss didn't 'make me mad' or cause this whole problem. And I know you said you really didn't care about the details of the situation, but I do need to fix it and somehow rework this whole scenario to explain and justify my behaviors—and save my reputation."

Jon shifted again and looked straight at Buddy.

"Buddy, I've worked so hard to manage my reputation, to make myself the perfect candidate for raises and promotions. How do I fix this? What can I blame for this disaster to save face and be that perfect team member again? How do I make all of this go away?"

"Do you know what my favorite command on a computer is, Jon?"

"To be honest, Buddy, I'm kind of surprised you use a computer," Jon interjected, not so much trying to be funny as honestly surprised. "I guess those board seats require it."

"Son," Buddy smiled, "Farmers and ranchers are some of the most prolific computer users I know. Attending webinars, projecting crop yield, herd management, financial projections. Now granted, farmers and ranchers are also most of the people I know, but still . . ." Buddy winked again.

"What command is it, Buddy?" Jon was getting impatient again.

"It's the 'undo' command. My big old fingers accidentally delete something I've been working on, and that undo command brings it all back. It completely erases my mistakes."

Jon was starting to connect with Buddy's analogies and was getting hopeful that he was about to hear about an undo command for his predicament.

Buddy again looked Jon in the eye. "Yes, sir, it's great. On computers. But, Jon, there is no undo command for the things we do in life; there is nothing we can do to make things that we've done magically go away.

"You recall that we were talking earlier about things we must accept and one of those things is our past. That acceptance doesn't just apply to our ancient past. It applies to this morning, as well."

Jon's face and spirit sunk even lower.

"You've heard me reference my good buddy, Truman. His full name is Dr. Herbert Truman Washington. Yeah, his dad liked presidents. Always believed he was directly descended from our first one. Maybe so. Names meant something to his dad. Anyway, he is a psychologist. Goes by Truman."

"Think I would, too," Jon threw in.

"You and me both," Buddy grinned. "I actually call him Dr. T. Well, there is something Dr. T. tells all of his patients, and friends, too, for that matter. He says, 'There are a whole lot of things I don't know, but there are a few things I absolutely know for sure. One of them is that love is the most powerful force in the universe; and a second one is that nobody can change what happened five years, five months, five weeks, or five minutes ago. The past is permanent.'"

Buddy paused and, for what was beginning to look like a rerun, he saw hopelessness flash across Jon's face.

"But, my friend, there are things we can do to change the impact of the past. Sometimes drastically, sometimes minutely. Sometimes physically, sometimes mentally. We can change the force of a painful past. We are not destined to be swept away by its currents. We have a paddle. We can, as we have been discussing, make choices."

"And what choice do I have to fix this mess?"

"Simple," Buddy said, with his face taking on more serious look.

"We talked about it earlier when I told you about my friend Josiah, remember?"

Jon thought about the earlier conversation, how Josiah was "so honest you could shoot craps with him over the phone." Josiah seemed like someone who took complete responsibility, with no excuses, for what he did.

Then Jon remembered the other thing he did.

"Apologize?" Jon asked, with a tone that indicated that he hoped he was wrong.

Buddy simply nodded.

The answer did not completely surprise Jon. In his earlier agitation, apologizing had not come to him as even a remote possibility. But as his brain had calmed while talking to Sofia and Buddy, the idea had wandered through his mind more than once.

"I kind of figured you were going to say that."

Buddy nodded again. "Jon, that means you've already become more self-aware, simply with that thought popping in your head. We make choices, Jon. And when that choice is a mistake, intentional or not, and creates consequences, intentional or not, and hurts others, intentional or not, a self-aware person apologizes. After all, it came out of their backpack."

Buddy kept looking Jon in the eye.

"Simply apologize. It's a key to a good marriage, good friendships, even good parenting. Apologize. Be vulnerable. And to do that well, you must be aware of what you've done and then take full, no-excuses responsibility."

Buddy went on. "If I leave my backpack in your way or whack you in the head with it while I'm walking down the aisle, I don't blame it on the fact that I forgot I had it on or that I may not travel much. I apologize. And then I learn from that mistake and change my behavior so I don't do it again; or I at least do it fewer times.

"I've said this more than once today, but every single one of us makes mistakes. Everyone. I've usually met my daily quota by my third cup of coffee, which, I might add, is very early in the day. People who live well, and even live with a greater sense of peace and comfort than most, are aware of themselves; when they make a mistake, they take full and immediate responsibility, no matter the cost. They own it, no excuses, and apologize, no matter the cost. Then they work to make changes, albeit imperfectly, to prevent the problem again—no matter the cost.

"And if you live your life that way, it all pays off."

In his head, Jon knew Buddy was right.

The idea was slowly getting to his heart.

He wasn't quite ready to admit it with his mouth.

Buddy knew that, too. And he knew the power of reflection: a mandatory practice for those growing in full awareness of their backpack.

And even though, when he was a pup, he had been labeled a "talker" by his mom, Buddy had also learned when to not fill a void in a conversation.

Jon finally broke the silence.

"So, if I take responsibility for what came out of my backpack and apologize, I will be able to regain my perfect team member status?" he asked hopefully—and doubtfully.

"Well, my friend, I'm sorry if I'm the first to break this to you," Buddy paused and grinned. "But you never were the perfect team member."

Jon's head and heart had known that, too.

"I am not trying to pile on, Jon. I am certainly not a fan of kicking a man while he's down."

"But?" Jon said, feeling his defenses start to rise.

"This is another *and*, Jon. Actually, it's two *and*s. The first one is, 'And don't get your boxers all in a wad and get defensive.' Feedback is a gift. Do you know the right response to any feedback we receive?"

Jon decided to not even guess and shook his head.

"It's 'thank you.' Someone took the time to tell me how I'm impacting them so I can get better. Even if it's not 100 percent accurate feedback, I shouldn't be defensive. I should simply say, 'Thank you.'"

That sank in, too.

"And the second *and*?"

"Jon, would you say that you are a competitive person? You like to win? People may even describe you as aggressive?"

Jon wasn't sure of the connection to apologizing, but he liked the fact that the conversation was getting to his strengths.

"100 percent!" Jon replied, with a sense of pride back in his voice.

"Then, my friend, in addition to apologizing to the right folks for, as you described it, this mess you made this morning, I would say you've got a whole list of people to apologize to."

Now Jon looked stunned.

"Yes, Jon, the second *and* is this: *and* I'd say you have some more apologizing to do. Aggressive, competitive people normally do."

"They tend to do a lot of whacking with their backpacks."

Chapter 31

Cecelia was coming down the aisle for the third time, this time collecting trash from passengers. Her look was stern, yet disconnected. She was doing a job, and not much more.

When she got to Jon and Buddy's aisle and coldly said, "Trash," as she held out the bag, Buddy again greeted her with a smile. As he dropped his coffee cup in the bag, he looked up at her and simply said, "Ma'am I apologize if I offended you earlier. Certainly didn't mean to do that. And thanks for all of your work today."

Cecelia paused for a moment, seemingly surprised, and almost reflexively said, "Thank you." Then she quickly turned to the folks across the aisle and kept on with her task.

Jon leaned toward Buddy. "Did you do that for my benefit?"

"Do what?"

"Apologize."

"Son, again, no offense, but at that moment I wasn't thinking about you. I was concerned with her. So, no sir. I apologized because it was the right thing to do," Buddy said, looking back over his shoulder just in time to notice a glance from Cecelia.

"But you stated earlier that she was low in self-awareness and you were simply trying to be nice. If your motives were good and she's not going to understand what you're doing anyway, why apologize?" Jon challenged.

Buddy grinned.

"Jon," Buddy paused. "Josiah, Dr. T, and my momma could sing three-part harmony on a verse they each recite all of the time. Independent of each other, mind you, but these are folks who, when they speak, I listen."

"And what was that? 'Do the right thing, regardless'?" Jon guessed.

"That's a good 'un, and they would all say that, too. But that's not what I was thinking of here. They would say: 'The only person you can control is you.'"

Buddy paused and looked upwards, thinking.

Jon did not want to interrupt. Though he remembered Grace saying that, too.

"People spend a lot of time trying to control other folks and even more time puffing up like a peacock because someone didn't do what they wanted them to. We judge people's backpacks. Get mad at their backpacks. Scream at them because their backpacks are in our way. But we rarely stop and ask ourselves, 'I wonder how *my* backpack is shaping and influencing this situation?' That's an important question, because it always is.

"Reminds me of a Wise Man who once asked, 'Why do you see the speck in your neighbor's eye, but do not notice the log that is in your own?'"

Jon kept listening. An hour ago, he would have stated, rather emphatically, that he was highly self-aware and faster than most at reading people and understanding what to do. Now, barreling along at almost 600 miles per hour, Jon was beginning to realize that when it came to true people skills and full self-awareness, he was barely taxiing on the runway.

"Jon, I don't apologize, or choose not to apologize, because of what the other person may or may not do. I can't control that. And because apologizing, in this situation and many situations, is the right thing to do, I do it. Regardless.

My backpack had a negative impact on another person, which was certainly not intentional but was still the result, so I own it—and apologize."

Jon continued to process, working to connect all of the dots of the backpack.

"Wait a minute on that, Buddy. Let's go back to the feedback conversation. Isn't giving critical feedback going to have negative impact on others? I mean, that's one reason people don't like to give feedback. They're afraid of hurting someone else's feelings. Or they water it down and over-filter it so much that the feedback becomes almost meaningless." Jon was starting to feel a little more confident in his people skills again. "That's why I think a lot of people aren't cut out for leading others. They're too nice. They'd rather be friends than give critical feedback."

Jon was getting bolder.

"So, what is a leader supposed to do, Buddy? Give feedback and then apologize for it? Seems like a vicious cycle that no one will ultimately take seriously."

Jon had been looking at the back of the seat in front of him while he was raising his point. It seemed to make him more confident to not look Buddy in the eye. When he turned back toward him, he was surprised to see that same big Texas grin.

"We're back watching that rodeo clown," Buddy laughed. Jon's eyebrows furled, but he had learned that if he waited a minute, Buddy would get to his point.

"Speaking of a few minutes ago, I mentioned John Wooden, one of the greatest, if not the greatest, college basketball coaches ever to step on a court."

"No argument from me," Jon replied.

"I kind of sped past him, but my point at the time was that the feedback he gave his players was continuous, not only once a year."

"I got that," Jon replied.

"From everything I've read about him, his players knew that he truly cared for them and that he wanted the absolute best for them. They would even say he loved them. One of Wooden's lessons of leadership was, 'Use the most powerful four-letter word.'[1] Do you know what that word was, Jon?"

Jon shook his head.

"Love."

Jon thought about that. Then it hit him. "But he also pushed them to get better. Is that the point?"

"Like before, it's more of an *and*. He loved his players *and* he pushed them to get better. It may be even more accurate to say that he pushed his players to get better *because* he loved them."

Jon thought about that, too.

"Have you heard about his pyramid of success?"

"I have," Jon replied.

"Coach Wooden had a box on that pyramid he called *alertness*,[2] which, now that I think about it, is a perfect fit for our backpack idea."

Jon noticed how Buddy had said *our*. His new friend wasn't too focused on *me*.

"If my old mind remembers correctly, he described alertness as always being aware, always observing, and always seeking to make you and the team better. Something like that."

"Are you saying that if people feel cared for, then they're never going to have their feelings hurt by critical feedback and it will just be one big party?" Jon asked, with a hint of sarcasm.

"No, sir. That's unicorns and rainbows. Even people you care for may rattle their six-shooter when you give them feedback they don't like. But if they know you don't care about them, then they are almost guaranteed to get honking mad, even if they don't show it, and completely discount whatever feedback you provided.

"Caring for folks well—encouraging, complimenting, and supporting them, knowing their stories—builds emotional equity and relational capacity to handle conflict. That earns you the right to give feedback. I don't give you feedback selfishly. I give it because I care for you. That's why I give it directly but supportively. And I take it the same way. And," Buddy grinned again, "as a reminder, when I receive feedback on my backpack, I should say ... ?"

"Thank you," Jon remembered from before.

Jon thought about that, too.

"People hear the term *critical* feedback, and they think it's like a movie critic whose job it is to point out everything that's wrong. That's not what I'm talking about. Not at all. The goal is always to be more coach than critic. And I can't go too far the other way and become a cheerleader whose job is to never give feedback. They believe 'We can do it, yes we can,' when you're down by 40 points with a minute left on the clock.

"We want to be the coach. A coach like Wooden."

They sat in silence before Buddy decided he needed to put a bow on this part of the conversation.

"Bottom line, my friend, is this: If I care about you, I want to know how my backpack is making your life better or worse, so I can do more or less as the situation warrants. And if I care about you, I want you to be the best, so I need to let you know everything I can about how I am being impacted by your backpack."

Chapter 32

J on was staring out the window. Thinking. Reflecting.

"Excuse me, sir."

Buddy and Jon both looked up at the young man standing next to them. It was the third flight attendant, Collin.

"I am sorry to bother you," the young man continued, "but are you Buddy?"

"He most definitely is," Jon said before Buddy could answer.

They all smiled.

"What can I do for you, young man? Is that Miss Sofia driving you like a rented mule?" Buddy asked, still smiling.

"What?! *Umm.* Oh . . . no. No, sir. Sofia's great."

"You're darn tootin' she is."

Collin regained his composure. "Actually, it was Sofia that said I should speak with you. Do you mind if I ask you a question?"

"Anything for Miss Sofia, young man. But you have to do something for me first."

Collin was taken back but pensively said, "Okay."

"You gotta tell us your name. You know I'm Buddy and this here's my good friend, Jon. And you are?"

"*Uhh*, Collin. My name's Collin. Sorry. All of the bantering confused me."

"Welcome to my planet, son. So, Collin, pleasure to meet you. Now fire away, figuratively, of course."

Collin took a breath and regained his composure.

"I'd like to ask you the same question I asked her. You see, I am fresh out of flight attendant training and—"

"A foal just getting his legs! I'd never have guessed."

"Buddy," Jon butted in, sternly, "You need to stop interrupting the poor guy."

Everything froze.

For a second.

"Just thought I'd give you a little critical feedback," Jon grinned.

"And I needed it," Buddy managed to get out through the laughter. "I was whacking this young man all over the place with my backpack!"

"Well, I've definitely found the fun row—and the confusing row," Collin said.

"That you have, young man, that you have. Now, fire it up. What question can we help you with?"

There was that *we* again.

"It's the same one I've been asking everybody I fly with. Even though you don't work for the airline—though I think it would be fun if you did—Sofia thought your opinion would be well worth my time."

Buddy nodded.

"So here it is: What's the best piece of advice you can give me for achieving long-term success in this job? I mean, I think I'm going to really enjoy the work. And I know I can meet all of the physical demands. Now I want to know how to fully succeed."

"Well, Collin, I think Sofia thought it would be good to ask folks outside of the airline industry, too, for one simple reason. Those things you just listed notwithstanding, the keys to success are the same in every job, from doctor to farmer, banker to teacher, rancher to whatever this guy here, does,"

Buddy nodded toward Jon. "And everybody else around and in between."

Buddy looked over at Jon. "I think you should answer this one."

"What?! Why should . . ." Jon started to protest, wondering how on earth he was going to boil down what he thought was the key to success in a job, any job, and worrying about how he was going to defend his answer in front of Buddy.

Then he looked at the ever-grinning Buddy . . . and he knew the answer.

"Collin," Jon began, "That is a great question. And the answer all starts with your backpack."

"*Huh?* I'm not sure . . ."

"I wasn't either," Jon continued, "but there are a few things about your backpack that you need to know and a few other things that you need to do. And as you work on those, you will be successful, in the right sense of the word, no matter where you go or what you try."

Jon spent the next 200 miles or so explaining the importance of knowing and owning your backpack. He explained how, first of all, you need to know which backpack is yours, and that included understanding your personality, your history, your strengths, your gaps, and all of the things that make you, *you.*

"Does that make sense, Collin?"

"It sure does. I love the backpack illustration. Believe me, I see it lived out every single flight of every single day."

"Especially the whacking, huh?" Buddy added.

"Especially the whacking," Collin agreed with a smile.

Jon went on to share that next in the backpack process was deciding what you were intentionally going to put in your backpack: your well-defined core values. Who you were going to be everywhere you went. With integrity.

"And to wrap up part one," Jon continued, and he went on to detail the importance of learning to accept the things about you and your life that you cannot change, even sharing that he finally had to accept that he had not, as he previously had thought, been the perfect teammate and employee.

He gave Buddy a wink.

"Ringer!" was all Buddy said.

Jon seamlessly moved on to the second backpack point: taking responsibility for it. Collin and Jon went back and forth with questions and answers until Collin—and a couple of surrounding passengers who had now joined in the conversation—had a grasp of the falsity of the phrase, "You make me so angry!" Then, Jon turned to the truth that "everything that comes out of my backpack is my responsibility, even if it dumped out when someone ran into me."

"And, Buddy?" Jon looked back at his friend. "You said at the beginning of our conversation that there were four things we needed to know about our backpacks. I just went over the first two: Know your backpack and take responsibility for your backpack. I believe that we've been talking about the third part of what we need to know: awareness of how our backpacks are impacting all of the people around us. Our discussion on the power of choice, making mistakes, apologizing, and getting good, honest feedback has all been about growing in the self-awareness of how my life, my backpack, is impacting others, correct?"

"Bull's-eye!" Buddy enthusiastically replied.

"Wow," Collin said. "That's all pretty amazing advice. I asked for one thing and got so much more! I need to go write it down before I forget it all."

"Yes and no," Buddy said.

Collin looked confused but waited.

"Yes, there were a lot of pieces, but it is still that one piece of advice you asked for. And that one piece of advice is . . .?"

Collin thought for a few seconds. "Own my backpack!"

Chapter 33

"Okay, Buddy. So, we're still missing one," Jon said. Conversations had continued between Collin, Jon, Buddy, and, now, several other passengers. Even Sofia made her way back to the row and joined in. They had been in smooth airspace for a while so the captain had turned off the seatbelt sign. The "put your headphones on and tune everyone else out" normal airline behavior was out the proverbial window.

At least in row 16.

It was Jon who had interrupted the conversations.

"Buddy, what was the fourth thing we need to know about our backpacks? After knowing it, owning it, and learning about how it impacts others, what's left? Why haven't you discussed that last one?"

Buddy smiled again. "Pardner, we've been discussing it all along."

Jon looked at him blankly. "Alright, Buddy. To use a phrase that could come from you, I'm sure I look like a deer in headlights. What am I missing?"

"I'd say 'confused as a goat on AstroTurf,' but we can go with the blinded deer."

Everybody smiled.

Addressing everybody, Buddy started, "Earlier Jon was telling me about the best boss he ever had, a gal by the name of Vera, who ran the grocery store where he worked as a teenager."

The group nodded.

Buddy turned toward Jon. "Jon, when I pushed you for why she was the best boss you ever had—beyond being smart, a hard worker, and a good businessperson—you said that there was a main reason she was the best."

Jon sat back in his seat and thought. He remembered the core value discussion, the fact that she was a very principled person, and said softly, "I knew she really cared for me."

"Bingo! And I shared that a major reason we practice self-awareness, and work to have a more positive impact on others, is because . . ."

"We care for them."

"*Uh-huh.* And I have been compelled to give you feedback and tell you the truth about how you're impacting me and others because . . ."

"You care about me."

"Exactly, because you can't care for someone and not tell them the truth. But be careful," Buddy said, looking around at everyone. "That truth can't be out of spite, or arrogance, or even with the 'I'm just sayin'' or 'Bless their little heart' qualifiers. We can't share feedback simply because it makes us feel better. And we should never be the feedback spokesperson. You know, the feedback that opens with, 'I've talked to other people and we all agree on this.'"

Several people nodded.

"We have to check our motives and make sure we are not sharing something with the intent to harm and then pretend like we weren't responsible for creating that harm. Excuse the metaphor, but in Texas we say, 'Don't pee on my boots and tell me it's raining.' Don't intentionally hurt me and pretend you meant it for good. We need to tell others the truth, but we need to make sure we speak the truth in . . ."

Buddy waited, as most folks smiled at the metaphor.

"In love," the woman in 15D responded.

"Yes, ma'am," Buddy nodded at her. "That doesn't mean we avoid sharing feedback that could create discomfort, if not even a little harm. Jon, I shared earlier that I've changed a lot since my younger years, and I don't mean physically. In my twenties, I was called a 'hothead' on more than one occasion. You can imagine I got defensive, I didn't like it, and, yes, it hurt.

"But I finally realized that it was true. And then I had to make a very important decision: Do I want to go through life being known as a hothead?"

Jon and others had trouble picturing Buddy that way, but they weren't going to challenge him.

"So, Jon, when we are discussing leaders that we respect who have had a direct positive impact on us, we know from the way they treated us that they . . ."

"Cared for us," a couple of voices said in unison.

"And one of the leadership lessons of the famed Coach Wooden is?"

"I'm guessing it's about caring for his players," the man in 16A responded.

Jon looked at them. "*Love* is the most powerful four-letter word," he filled in.

"And finally," Buddy continued, looking directly at Jon, "The number-one thing my ole buddy Dr. T tells all of his patients is . . ."

"Well, the number-two item is that no one can change the past," Jon said. He thought for a moment and then remembered. "And the first is, 'Love is the most powerful force in the universe.'"

No one doubted the truth of that statement.

"So," Jon continued, "the fourth thing I need to know or do is love people with my backpack?"

Everyone looked at Buddy and waited.

"There are probably lots of ways you could say it: I need to love people with what comes out of my backpack, like with my words and my actions. Even when I speak truth that may bring a little pain, it still needs to come from love.

"Another way to say it is: Loving people means making sure my backpack helps them and doesn't hinder them, so I pay attention to those around me. I should ultimately work, albeit imperfectly, to not whack people with my backpack," Buddy said looking directly at Jon.

Buddy paused. "At the core of it all is genuinely and authentically loving myself and others." Buddy paused again. "All others. That has to be the motivation to do anything at all with my backpack."

"I have to want to be the best person that I can be," Jon filled in.

"And I have to ultimately want what is best for others," Sofia finished.

"This may be a little cowboy blunt, but if you don't genuinely care for others, then there's not a lot I can do for you."

"How come?" someone asked.

"Well," Buddy continued, "I can love you regardless because my choosing to care for you is not dependent on your caring for me. You can be a jerk and I can still care for you. No offense." Buddy winked.

"But if you honestly don't give a horse's hair about how your backpack affects others, good or bad, then the only person you really care about is you. And I have found that if you only care about you, you pretty much have zero motivation to change."

Jon asked, "Is this one of the other things that really 'gets your quills up,' Buddy? One is people don't think they need to learn anything and the other is people who demonstrate they don't care for others?"

Buddy grinned. "Lucky, I would say you are already getting better at paying attention to others and what they're feeling. That is it, exactly!"

Sofia jumped back in. "And there is the additional irony that those same people are the unhappiest people on the planet. I've never met a self-focused person who was happy." People nodded in agreement.

"When my buddy Dr. T is asked, 'What's the biggest problem in relationships?' he simply says: 'People.'"

Now there were confused faces almost all around.

"Because people," Sofia picked up the conversation, "are inherently selfish."

Now it was starting to all make sense.

"We're not all jerks who could care less about what our backpacks do to others," Buddy continued. "Still, we all have to battle our selfishness, that stubborn desire to let our backpacks be about *our* convenience, regardless of the inconvenience to others."

Buddy glanced back at Jon.

"Kind of like me putting the middle tray table down to try and keep this seat empty, even if it meant someone else would have to move further back in the plane," Jon added, somewhat embarrassed, yet acknowledging his own behavior.

Sofia and Buddy exchanged a quick glance.

"And what do y'all think is the antidote to selfishness?" Buddy said, pulling a little bit of the spotlight off of Jon.

"I'd say it's love," shared the woman in 15D.

"Yes, ma'am. You can bet your last dollar on that truth."

Buddy looked back at Jon.

"Jon, number four—and this is *the* fact of life, the final thing we need to learn in order to live and enjoy this ole life of ours to the fullest—is to love others well with our whole backpack."

Chapter 34

J on thought.

He had been listening.

And learning.

And wondering.

He looked down at his now somewhat unfamiliar backpack.

"Buddy," he began, "I've got another question, and I think you're the one smart enough to answer it."

"Still feel dumber than a fence post most of the time," Buddy interrupted.

Jon grinned. "I'm certainly not a historian," he continued, "but it seems that since the beginning of humankind, the poets, philosophers, theologians, and even musicians have been trying to tell us that love is the answer. So, I think you're in good company when you say that *the* fact of life is to love others well . . . with our backpack."

Now the crowd was fully focused on Jon.

He continued. "I don't presume to speak for everybody, but I think we can all agree that people who love other people well are great to be around."

It was a subject that was easy to build consensus on; everyone nodded.

"And as I think about it," Jon said, "People who love people well can change the world. *Umm*, like Dr. King, or . . ."

"Gandhi," said one.

"Mother Teresa," said another.

"The Biography Channel listed Jesus as the most influential person in history, and He was all about love," another added.

"My first-grade teacher," said Collin.

People looked at him with a look that said they wanted to know more.

Collin blushed. "The short story is that I come from a very messed-up family. My father abandoned us, my mother had drug problems. Then I met Miss Minett. I can't tell you much about the subjects we covered, but I can remember how much she loved me."

A tear came to Collin's eye. Everyone wanted him to go on, but they all understood that they already knew everything they needed to know.

Jon let that hang in the air for a moment, and then realized it was a great segue to his question. "Buddy, the problem, as I see it, is that there don't seem to be too many Miss Minetts in the world."

"And there seem to be fewer by the day," said the woman in 15B.

More nods.

"Buddy, my new old friend, I get on a lot of planes and the whacking doesn't seem to be getting any better or any less frequent. And the love is almost nonexistent. How do we change that?" Jon finished, doubtful there was an answer.

Everyone waited on Buddy.

"You know, folks, I was reading an article awhile back—and, please, no comments about being surprised I can read," Buddy grinned. "I had a good first-grade teacher, too." Buddy winked at Collin. "The article was in a science journal describing how empathy between folks had decreased over the last 30 years. It's a durn shame."

Nobody looked surprised.

"And, of course, they had theories as to why. Any guesses?" Buddy asked.

Collin started. "People are scared of talking to strangers because there seems to be a lot of strange individuals, or they don't want to be thought of as a strange individual. Present company excluded," Collin smiled.

More laughter.

"I certainly fit that bill," Buddy said. "Other ideas?"

"People are in too much of a hurry."

"Or too wrapped up in themselves."

"And too wrapped up in whatever they're doing with whatever devices they're staring at," added Sofia.

"Right you all are," Buddy began. "And Miss Sofia highlighted the core behaviors pointed out by the scientists: the increased social isolation brought on by the ever-expanding media world. Some people don't see it as, 'It's me and my backpack to help the world,' but rather, 'It's me and the devices I carry in my backpack against the world.'"

People nodded at that, too.

"Now before y'all think I'm anti–social media or don't like phones because I'm older than Moses' daddy, that is not the case. I've got the best dumb phone that money can buy."

Everyone was falling in love with the old cowboy.

"What I am anti is the behavior that has become exceedingly worse because of this increased isolation. I'm sure y'all have some examples of that."

They came from everybody, one after another.

From unfriending to cyberbullying to name calling to vicious character attacks and unwanted revenge photos, everyone had either heard of a situation or experienced one themselves. Hateful attacks, verbal and otherwise, seemed to be a daily staple of newsfeeds.

"Isolation makes it too easy to be mean to people," Sofia said after the sharing died down. "Even in the cramped quarters of a plane, people remain isolated and disconnected so it is easy to judge the mom with the crying baby, the guy who needs a seatbelt extension, or the person whacking people with their backpack. Without empathy, we don't try to feel what they're feeling so there's no social connection."

Buddy let Sofia's wise words hang in the air.

"And without empathy, it's extremely difficult to get to that most important fact of life." Buddy looked over at Jon. "That fourth thing about our backpack."

"Loving people well," Jon added.

Buddy nodded.

"You see, folks, without empathy, people simply do not work to understand others and connect with their world; they fail to put themselves in the other person's place and feel what they're feeling."

Buddy again paused.

"And without love, people aren't kind to one another; we do not demonstrably work to care for others. We don't respond with empathy and choose to make other people's journeys just a little bit better. And without both," Buddy paused one more time, "the world is a lonely, hurting, angry place; and people fail to become the people they were designed to be."

No one disagreed.

"Now folks," Buddy grinned again, "I'm not trying to tip over the outhouse here, but I do feel the need to bring this full circle. Let's say you're walking down the aisle here and unbeknownst to you, you're whacking people with your backpack. Like my buddy, Jon, here."

Jon simply shook his head—but smiled.

"All of a sudden you discover that fact because some poor fella says, '*Ouch!*' Now what do you do?"

Several answers came in at once. "Apologize."

"Say, 'I'm sorry.'"

"Say, 'Excuse me.'"

"And why is that?" Buddy asked.

"Because you realized your hurt someone," came the reply.

"*Hmmm*," Buddy started.

"Well, that's the socialized-by-our-first-grade-teacher response, which isn't bad, mind you. We like our first-grade teachers," Buddy winked at Collin again. "But you really apologized because you have empathy, because you understand what it's like to be on the other end of the whacking! And once you realize what you've done, with love and compassion you alter your behavior so you don't whack anyone else. Make sense?"

Nods all around.

"Collin," Buddy continued, "why do you airline folk refer to people on planes as '*souls?*'"

"It's the quickest way to describe the total number of living, breathing people on board. You don't separate out passengers from crew. We are all fellow human beings."

Buddy let that sink in, too.

"Jon, in answer to your question about how to change the low empathy and even lower expressions of love, we must first see all of our fellow passengers on this journey of life as souls. We are all fellow-human beings. We are more alike than we are different. Reminding ourselves of that increases empathy. Putting down our phones and talking to other souls increases empathy. Next, we act on that empathy and practice compassion.

"Folks, that kind of behavior can seem as scarce as grass around a hog trough, but even this little band of new friends right here can have a huge impact. Do good unto others. We learned that in first grade, too. And this isn't just cowboy truth. There is some serious science around all of the benefits to both the giver and the receiver of compassion. The more you practice random acts of kindness, paying for people's coffee, leaving a big tip, writing thank-yous, offering kind words, letting someone pull in front of you in traffic, holding doors, helping others with luggage, encouraging others, and on and on, the happier you are—and other souls are enjoying life more as well.

"The happiest, most fulfilled folks on the airplane of life are those who just plain-ole do everything they can to help other people with their backpacks."

Chapter 35

As if on cue, the plane hit some turbulence and the pilot turned the seatbelt sign on. Cecelia, who seemed to be hiding in the galley, made the announcement. Collin and Sofia ushered folks back to their seats.

From Sofia's perspective, not much had changed with Cecelia's aggressiveness, which could be heard in her tone and volume on the PA.

That wasn't true for the souls around row 16.

Though most were now sitting in silence, they were all thinking.

Thinking about their backpacks. And what they were going to do with them.

The conversation between Buddy and Jon now turned to what Buddy referred to as "earning your spurs."

If you're going to live with a loving backpack, there were some hard decisions to make; there were some tough conversations to be had. There were some life changes that needed to occur.

The wisdom of the backpack was not given; it was earned.

And it started with a decision.

"Jon, my daddy used to say, 'To decide not to decide, is to decide not to.'"

Jon thought about that.

"We can't just go on thinking about what we're going to do with our backpacks. We have to intentionally decide what we are going to do, and then do it, correct?" Jon asked confidently.

"Another ringer!" Buddy replied.

"So," Buddy continued, "the questions that remain are all about what you and I are going to do with our backpacks."

For the remainder of the flight, the two new friends went back through each and every topic Buddy had promised to return to.

On personalities: Buddy explained that we study them to understand ourselves better and to recognize how others may be wired differently than us. But personalities are never an excuse for bad behavior. Buddy shared stories from his younger days when he used to blame his hot temper on his fiery personality. And on other people, of course. Neither is acceptable.

On why we behave the way we do: There is a reason. And paying attention to exactly what we are feeling in the moment is the way to choose the right behaviors—even amidst stress. Knowing we are stressed and why we are stressed leads us to make self-aware choices to deal with that stress. And our stress level will lower.

On what should be stressful . . . and what should not: Buddy walked Jon through how stress is a neurological response to a threat. In the animal kingdom, the stress response is usually a matter of life and death. For humans, that's not so much the case. Souls have the unique ability, only shared by certain members of the ape species, to get stressed about things that are not life and death, things like missing a plane or losing a job.

On life's tempo: Jon had complained earlier that he never had time to sit and reflect, as Buddy had done. Buddy pointed out that there was one person ultimately in charge of Jon's schedule, especially his mental pace, in spite of setbacks like traffic and alarms—and that person was Jon.

On learning about all of this being fun: They had covered that one, but Buddy reminded Jon that there were many mistakes yet to come, for both of them. However, it can still be fun to learn to hurt fewer people and take better care of ourselves as we grow in awareness of our backpacks.

Finally, they reviewed Buddy's facts of life, including a few that Buddy had not shared with Jon previously.

Buddy's Facts of Life

◆ "People need friends."

◆ "Everybody's got baggage."

◆ "You cannot always choose what happens to you, but you can choose how you respond to what happens to you."

◆ "No matter the circumstances, I am responsible for my reaction, including my anger."

◆ "Do the right thing regardless of how others respond."

◆ "Don't try to make everyone happy—or you'll make yourself miserable."

◆ "Know that *not* everybody is going to love you, much less like you."

◆ "Do not live your life worried about what other people think of you."

◆ "Get out of your own world and be nice to others, regardless of what other people may think of you for doing so."

◆ "You must be able to laugh at yourself."

◆ "Words matter. Choose them wisely."

◆ "We all make emotional and physical mistakes."

◆ "You don't fully know what it's like to be me, and I don't fully know what it's like for you to be with me."

◆ "Our personalities, our parents, our past, our certain peculiarities are all things we must accept."

◆ "With no or even limited self-awareness, you are constantly and unknowingly impacting others, sometimes positively and often negatively, with your backpack."

♦ "The only folks who are really stuck are those who don't think they need feedback."

And they reviewed the four things we all need to know when it comes to our backpacks.

1. "We need to know exactly which one is ours, decide what we want in it, and accept it."
2. "We must take responsibility for it—all of it—at all times."
3. "We need to understand exactly how it impacts anybody and everybody around us."
4. "In order to live and enjoy this ole life of ours to the fullest we need to learn to love others well with everything that is in, and comes out of, our backpacks."

They even talked about why Buddy referred to Jon by the nickname Lucky. It's all about perspective. Science had also demonstrated that developing a habit of gratitude was a key to a happy, enjoyable life. Taking the time to reflect on and write down things we are grateful for gives us a sense of wonder, joy, and peace. All things that Jon was missing at the beginning of his day.

Buddy wanted Jon to know that if he took time to count his blessings, he would understand how lucky he really was.

Jon's head was swimming. They discussed more thoughts and ideas than, in Buddy's words, "you can shake a stick at."

"Buddy," Jon began, calmly and thoughtfully.

Buddy nodded and waited.

"It's time to get back to my mess. Don't you think?"

"Yes, sir, my friend. I do believe the time is right."

Buddy gave another big ole Texas grin and said, "Let's talk about what you are going to choose to do with your backpack."

What Now?

Now that you know all about your backpack, what are you going to do?

And what should Jon do?

What are his next steps with:

- His wife, Grace
- His boss
- The email referring to his boss as the PHB
- His children, Jaxx, Annalise, and Lilly
- The client he is flying out to see
- His coworkers
- Buddy
- Himself

I am not going to answer those questions because there is no one exact right answer for each of those relationships. Of course, there are what I would consider some wrong answers, but that shouldn't surprise you. Hopefully you now understand what those wrong answers look like. However, when it comes to understanding and using our backpacks in the pursuit of our best selves while loving others well, there are choices.

There are always choices with our backpacks.

There is a growing body of leadership literature stressing the importance of self-awareness, which, as this book has discussed, includes a healthy other-awareness, as well. Many have claimed—and I would wholeheartedly agree—that this type of self-awareness is the most important leadership skill of all.

My questions now are: What do *you* believe? And what are *you* going to do about it?

It is, most definitely, up to *you*.

You will not be surprised after reading *The Backpack* that I have been very purposeful about the character names I have chosen. Names have meaning and I am sure that you have picked up on some of them.

Here is a review of a few of the characters and the reasons their names were chosen.

Jon (and every variation of John) is always on the top five list of most common male names. No offense to all of my friends named Jon/John. There are a lot of you. For *The Backpack*, the commonness of the name Jon is analogous to the commonness of people who lack self-awareness. There are a lot those people, too. There is work to do.

Sofia means *wisdom*. Wisdom is not knowledge; it is the application of knowledge. Sofia understood what she needed to do to take care of herself so she could be her best—and she did it. She was therefore more than competent and qualified to share her wisdom with others, and she did it with grace and kindness.

Giving grace to another person is offering them the gift of unearned kindness and forgiveness. We all need that gift. In *The Backpack*, Grace offers grace continually to Jon, along with a hefty dose of loving wisdom. Both are critical in healthy relationships.

Collin means *victory*. In our story, Collin wants to learn and grow in order to give himself every chance to succeed in his new career. He has an open heart as well as a mind focused on learning and growing. And he knows that a growth-oriented attitude will bring him victory.

Cecelia means *blind*. A lack of self-awareness makes us emotionally blind to those around us and, as such, we become people who are completely wrapped up in ourselves. We never get out of our own backpacks or care about the pain we inflict on others. Again, my apologies to anyone named Cecelia; I am not saying there are too many of you. But we do have too many people who are blind to themselves and their impact on others. Hopefully, they will choose to grow.

Any Harry Potter fans know that the name Dumbledore has meaning, but I only picked it because I think it's a cool name for a dog.

Buddy means *friend*. As Buddy himself would say: 'Nuff said.

The names of the other minor characters have meaning, as well. I encourage you to research those if you're interested.

For those of you who wonder which character represents me, well, I am Buddy and I am also Jon.

I try everyday, albeit imperfectly, to be a good friend. Yet there have also been days, if not years, when I was completely wrapped up in myself and didn't pay attention to anyone else.There are many times where I take full responsibility for me; and there are still times when I blame my problems and my emotions on others. There is still work to do on me.

I believe I have channeled Sofia on occasion and shared a little wisdom here and there.

And I have been blessed to be married to Amy, who embodies Grace daily, for over 30 years.

In other words, I am a fellow-struggler with you on this journey of life, as we all figure out our backpacks.

I can sincerely say that since the idea of *The Backpack* came to me, I think about my backpack, literally and figuratively, all of the time.

Especially every time I get on a plane. And I get on a lot of planes.

Every story I've told about people whacking other people with their backpacks I've seen firsthand—and many of them

I've experienced *first-hand*. And I have been on the other end, too, as the one doing the whacking.

But, like Sofia, I try to get a little wiser with every trip, be it a trip to the coffeeshop or a trip at 30,000 feet. Every day is an opportunity to learn more about me. And every day is an opportunity to care for others a little bit better than the day before.

I will never know every single thing about my own backpack nor control it perfectly. But I can, with good feedback, continually get better at dealing with my constraints and, as a result, ploddingly reduce the negative impact I have on others.

I may not be able to help everyone in the world, but I can have a positive influence on everyone who crosses my path.

As I've gotten older, I strive to evaluate the success of my days with one simple question. It is a question that Buddy would ask himself: *Did I love people well today?*

I hope you join me and many others on this journey of self-awareness and loving others well. It will make the world a better place.

The choice is yours.

It's your backpack.

Notes

Chapter 2

1. Markman, Howard J., Scott M. Stanley, and Susan L. Blumberg. *Fighting for Your Marriage* (Jossey-Bass: San Francisco, 2010).
2. Thanks to Dave Lindsey, Founder and Chairman of DEFENDERS, Inc., for sharing his packing SOP.

Chapter 18

1. Gottman, John, and Nan Silver. *The Seven Principles for Making Marriage Work* (Three Rivers Press: New York, 1999).

Chapter 19

1. Eurich, Tasha. "What Self-Awareness Really Is," *Harvard Business Review*, January 4, 2018.

Chapter 20

1. Lencioni, Patrick. "Make Your Values Mean Something," *Harvard Business Review*, July 2002.

Chapter 31

1. Wooden, John, and Steve Jamison. *Coach Wooden's Leadership Game Plan for Success* (McGraw-Hill Education: New York, 2009), 107.
2. Ibid., 36.

Acknowledgments

P eople say that writing a good book is a community effort. That's true. More importantly, living a good life is a community effort. I'm grateful I have a great community for both.

First and forever, I am grateful for Amy, my bride of over 30 years—you are my cheerleader, coach, critic, and best friend. You make my life and my writing far better than they would ever be without you. May there be many more opportunities to write on the beach—while toasting sunset!

I am forever grateful for our children, Caleb, Grace, and Austin. As you each make your own phenomenal path in life, may you always remember that the porch light is on, you're on the favorites list so you can call anytime of the day or night, and that you are each responsible for your own backpacks. Never forget that you are loved deeply by us and by God. And never forget that you were made to love others and make this world a better place.

I am grateful for Kurt & Vickie, Glenn & Nancy, Craig & Julie B., Steve & Bobbi, and Tom & Julie P., our faithful community group. Thank you for the love, prayers, and support, and for going through the ups and downs of life together. May ocean-life be frequent.

I am grateful for my immediate family and close friends: all of the Gardners, Schocks, Vern & Mary, Scat, 50+ year Texas friends, and so many more. My friendship cup runneth over.

I am grateful for my work family and friends at the Flippen Group! It is an honor to be with you on our shared mission to bring out the best in people around the world. Thank you